THE NEW
Elevator Pitch

THE NEW ELEVATOR PITCH
© 2012 By
Chris Westfall
ALL RIGHTS RESERVED

Cover art design by Christina Isabel Gray

ISBN: 978-0-9854148-0-1
First Printing: 2012
MARIE STREET PRESS
5930 Royal Lane Suite E-373 Dallas, TX 75230
Tel +1 214.519.8033

http://thenewelevatorpitch.com
http://mariestreetpress.com

Printed by
Lightning Source
1246 Heil Quaker Blvd.• La Vergne, TN USA 37086
(615) 213-5815• lightningsource.com

Advance Praise for
The NEW Elevator Pitch

"In today's environment of overstimulation, sometimes the most challenging task is simply to capture someone's attention. Whether you are seeking a job or even a first date, creating a compelling first interaction with someone is deceptively difficult. *The New Elevator Pitch* is a critical resource to help you create breakthrough communications when it matters the most."

> **– Carol Roth**
> **Recovering investment banker & New York Times**
> **bestselling author of** *The Entrepreneur Equation*

"A journey of a thousand miles doesn't start with a single step - it starts with a single story. Get clear on your message, and watch where the journey takes you! Highly recommended!"

> **– Dean Lindsay**
> **Author of** *The Progress Challenge* **and** *Cracking the Networking CODE*

"Whether you have to pitch yourself and your ideas on a regular basis or you're simply wanting to clarify your unique value proposition, the time you spend working through the exercises in Chris Westfall's fun and practical new book will prove indispensable to your business success."

> **– Michael Neill**
> **Author of** *You Can Have What You Want* **and the Effortless Success audio program, www.supercoach.com**

"I have met few people that can inspire the way Chris Westfall can."

> **– Dan Newman**
> **The Millennial CEO**

"In business, it's all about qualifying. Chris Westfall's book shows you how to open the door to get to the close! In order to have a conversation you must draw the prospect in. Chris helps you do just that. Trust me when I tell you this sales book is different and his techniques will work!"

– **Lois Creamer**
Author of *Working Smart, Not Hard*

"Today, opening is the new closing. You can't afford not to know what Chris teaches. Don't just read the book! Study it and apply it now!"

– **S. Anthony Iannarino**
President, Solutions Staffing and Adjunct Faculty, Capital University http://www.thesalesblog.com

"Chris is the truth!!! He comes to the heart of the matter - Brilliant!"

– **Josie Aiello**
Universal Recording Artist, President and CEO of Dream Garden Music

"If you're in business, life's a pitch! But, the in your face, old-school pitch is repulsive. Thankfully *The NEW Elevator Pitch* nails it...and gives you the most important skill if you need to tell it to sell it. Awesomeness!"

– **Jason Bax**
Entrepreneur and Pitchman; Founder of Pitchmasters.org

"What sets Westfall apart is his commitment to authenticity. Unlike cookie-cutter "how to" books, Westfall genuinely wants us to speak from the heart and be true to ourselves as we craft the message that will empower us to succeed. If you want to lead the way with your message, this is a must-read book."

– **Lisa Petrilli**
CEO of C-Level Strategies, Inc. and Harvard Business Review Blogger

"It doesn't matter how important your message is if you don't get it out there with a compelling delivery! In *The New Elevator Pitch*, Chris Westfall shows you exactly how he does it. Follow his simple, essential steps to inspire those three magical words that will transform your career: 'Tell me more...'"

    – Ted Coine
        Author, speaker, Co-founder of the Switch and Shift blog
        (http://switchandshift.com)

"Everyone thinks they can communicate well. Sounds coming from your mouth, words on a page or an upside down triangle in a PowerPoint presentation is not a guarantee of effective communication. *The New Elevator Pitch* is clear, concise and direct. This book is a unique and brilliant approach to successful communication."

    – Joel Zeff
        National speaker, workplace expert, humorist and author
        of *Make the Right Choice: Creating a Positive, Innovative,*
        and Productive Work Life

"This book is a must-read for anyone who believes in the power of humanized branding for sustainable career growth in today's digital age. Chris Westfall is living his brand in a unique voice."

    – Meghan M. Biro
        CEO and Founder, TalentCulture

"Chris gets it... being persuasive is about building relationships, and delivering the right message at the right time."

    – Ted Rubin
        Chief Social Marketing Officer of Collective Bias and
        Author of *Return on Relationship*™

"Chris has a gift for defining what the listener needs to hear, distilling the essence of the message and helping clients to find their voice by connecting all the dots."

    – Douglas Pond
        Chief Commercial Officer for Opportunity International,
        Mozambique

"I am a seasoned communication prof and a public speaker... and, at times, even I struggle with brevity and succinctness in my message! Chris's book is a great reminder for veterans like me, and for anyone who wants to develop a "captivating core" of what they are trying to get across. The book is written in an open, welcoming, conversational tone. Readers will be able to implement the recommendations the second they put it down."

    – **Ellen B. Bremen**
       Author of *Say This, NOT That to Your Professor: 36 Talking Tips for College Success*

For Lisa, Ruby and Noli –
and for anyone who has a story to tell.

Table of Contents

Foreword by

Jeffrey Hayzlett

Business & Marketing Authority, Bestselling Author & Sometime Cowboy

Quite frankly, I'm amazed at the number of intelligent people I know in business who don't have a decent elevator pitch.

I've sat through thousands of sales presentations with 100 + Power Point slides and wondered afterward, "I don't get it. What is it you do?" Forget the pretty slides showing your biggest clients, the awards you received last year....what's your unique value proposition ?...what's the value you're going to provide to me as a potential customer? And make it quick!

It's time to rethink our sales strategy; it's time to drive change and grow.

The simple fact of the matter is: no matter what your occupation, you sell something every day. Maybe it's new technology, or brand management, or just a great idea about where to go to dinner in New York City (believe me,

THE NEW ELEVATOR PITCH

I can run that one down for you). Change and success in business is like breathing and fogging the mirror; you've got to do it to survive, and it's a constant. If you don't-- you're dead.

Sales and growth are the only way to build the future of your business. It's the only way to engage others in your ideas, your brand, your YOU. What's the point of driving change in your personal life, your professional life, your company or your team, if you can't get out there and build on your success?

Do you want to engage, persuade and influence? Guess what: you don't have a choice! You have to do all three, if you want to lead, drive change, and grow profits.

My first book, *The Mirror Test*, outlines my concept of the 118 Pitch – a modern version of the traditional elevator pitch. The 118 Pitch originates from the premise you have 8 seconds to hook them and 110 seconds to drive it home. The response to the need for a 118 Pitch – where you promote and sell what your company offers in the span of an elevator ride– was tremendous!

Simply, your 118 Pitch must do the following:

- Grab the attention of your prospect.
- Convey who you are.
- Describe what your business offers.
- Explain the promises you will deliver on.

FOREWORD BY JEFFREY HAYZLETT

Running the Gauntlet, my most recent book, further emphasizes the significance of developing a powerful and concise 118 pitch. Anyone in business must lead change by eating, living, breathing and saying who you are and what you do. Be clear on the message that exemplifies everything about your business - and you - in a way that grabs my attention!

You know what grabs attention? Getting back to your core, your authentic message. A brand isn't only what you put on a cow. In business, a brand is a promise delivered. Deliver on your promise! Understanding your most basic message is the best way to drive change.

In my own business, I challenge my team to be clear on the value we deliver. In your own 118 Pitch, be clear on the value you offer, get others engaged, and embrace change.

Passion is no substitute for planning, and expressing your value in 118 seconds is your mission. Doesn't matter if your business is rounding up cattle or sitting behind a desk in the C-Suite– know it well or your offer will be buried in the noise of everyday business. You can't close because you haven't even opened the conversation.

When you know your story, and educate your prospect with radical transparency, communicate it with authenticity, your clients and associates feel it. They become excited, engaged and eventually evangelists for your company and brand.

For those of you who don't already know, Chris Westfall won our very first "118 Pitch Contest." (Check it out on YouTube). Chris' pitch blew me away. It's clear he understands and demonstrates the effectiveness of a strong 118 Pitch. He truly gets it! Learn more, saddle up and read on my friend.

Jeffrey Hayzlett

The NEW
Elevator Pitch

Think about the most important person in your life right now.

Beyond your family and your romantic interests, there are friends and partners that want to know more about you – about your skills, talents, goals and ideas. Communicating effectively with the important people in your life can create some incredible results, if you know how to do it. What would it mean to you to be able to engage your clients, Board Members, or potential employers in a story that was persuasive and inspiring? What could you create, through a deeper and richer connection with your most important person?

Anything of any value is created through others. From relationships to revolutionary new products, communication skills are the key to advancing your ideas. Would you like to know how to engage and influence your most important person? How about all of your customers, Facebook friends, and more?

THE NEW ELEVATOR PITCH

When it comes time to connect with the people that matter, you have many tools at your disposal. From twitter to match.com, we have more ways than ever to connect. But, unfortunately, we're not making very real connections. Electronic friends are great, but what about the connections that go beyond the world of social media? What's your story, when the conversation really has to matter?

The NEW Elevator Pitch isn't really a "pitch" at all – it's a method for starting important conversations. Beyond the chatter, when it comes time to get down to business you have to have a method for conveying your ideas. Whether you tweet it or tell it, you have to have a story that's strong – otherwise, it's lost in the noise. Today, the conversation often starts online – making it more important than ever to understand what your story is, before you share it with the entire World Wide Web.

Traditionally, a "pitch" has been something that has some aggressive connotations - for example, selling something to someone, whether they want it or not. The NEW Elevator Pitch isn't about pushy tactics or "speechifying" someone into submission. The NEW Elevator Pitch isn't just a two-minute speech. It's a method of communication, designed for the digital age.

I wrote this book because I believe that you need to be heard. I believe that your story matters – whether it's a story about a social cause, a new product, or just a creative idea about customer service. Your message –and how you tell it - is important to me.

As the national elevator pitch champion, I've had the opportunity to work with thousands of executives, students and Fortune 1000 organizations on the application of powerful communication skills. In my experience, everyone I've worked with has one thing in common. We all have a powerful desire to create real connections. That connection begins with a powerful conversation – a conversation that I call The NEW Elevator Pitch.

Making a connection is what I try to do every time I work with a client, and every time I speak to an audience. I've come to understand that the human condition is about a human connection. You owe it to yourself to understand how to navigate that connection via effective communication. You deserve to understand the secrets of influence, persuasion, and interaction – without it feeling like some artificial "pitch."

Rare is the occasion in life when we can script our remarks. The NEW Elevator Pitch shows you how you can build a framework for your story – the story where your listener says, "Tell me more..."

You'll hear a lot about "Tell me more..." in the upcoming pages. I believe that the best communication is judged not by what you say, but by what your listener *does when you are done.* The ongoing dialogue is the sign of connection – the conversation continues, and you get closer to your goals and desires. Your communication isn't judged by how well you pronounce your vowels, or your gesture patterns, or the cohesive structure of your speech. No, it's judged based on what someone does when you finish speaking. Creating that compelling call to action, in two minutes or less, is the objective of The NEW Elevator Pitch.

For the people who are important to you, it's important that you can communicate clearly. You have to be clear on who you are, what you're about, and what you need. The people around you want to know your "Why?" – in other words, they need to understand the things that are important to you, and how they can get involved and engaged in your ideas.

Jeffrey Hayzlett, author of *The Mirror Test*, explains that the NEW Elevator Pitch is 118 seconds long – about the length of the average elevator ride in New York City. Using that two-minute benchmark, The NEW Elevator Pitch will provide you with a framework for telling your story. The NEW Elevator Pitch is concise, compelling, and authentic – not gimmicky, schmoozy or forceful. Someone important to you wants to know more about your thoughts and ideas... Are you ready to start the conversation?

Origins
The original "elevator pitch" comes from the studio days of Hollywood, when a screenwriter would

(supposedly) catch an unsuspecting executive on an elevator ride. There, with his prey trapped within the confines of the elevator, the screenwriter would 'pitch' an idea to the decision-maker, in 30, 60, or even 118 seconds.

How realistic do you think it would be that an executive would say "yes" to a screenplay, in an elevator – even if the pitch were as simple as "Snakes on a Plane"?

The urban legend of the elevator pitch was born.

Times have changed since the studio days of Hollywood. Changed. A. Lot.

Nobody's waiting for the elevator anymore.

"Why would I talk to a TV executive at this point, and ask them what they think? If I have this idea for a TV show, I can just put it up on the Internet." – Jerry Seinfeld

The idea of the "elevator pitch" – a short, persuasive speech designed to sell something in the length of an elevator ride – is out of date. In fact, if you're thinking of "pitching" anything, you're making a mistake. The NEW Elevator Pitch isn't a pitch at all.

The Update

No matter what your chosen profession, you have to convince others to follow your ideas. You have to influence the folks you work with, live with, and care about. You have to get others engaged in what you are saying. Engagement is not a "pitch" – it's influence. Engagement is a connection. Engagement can start via online tools and social media but it really comes home when you deliver your message in person.

Jeffrey Hayzlett understands the importance of engagement, and the '118' pitch is the updated version. After all, why just "give a speech" when you can deliver a message?

The old elevator pitch is a relic from a bygone era. The idea of speechifying someone into submission, or into a buying decision, is about as relevant as a buggy whip. The NEW Elevator Pitch is still persuasive, still brief, and still compelling – but designed for the way we speak, engage and interact today. The NEW Elevator Pitch is a fresh and modern message that focuses on you – your story, your desires and your style. Most importantly, the NEW Elevator Pitch is about creating action - the kind of outcomes you want from the people you need. Breakthroughs happen when you know how to make what matters, matter. If you're ready to be heard, you're ready for the NEW Elevator Pitch.

The NEW Elevator Pitch Demands CLARITY
What makes a great elevator pitch?

The best elevator pitch you (or anyone else) can possibly deliver will focus on the most important person in the room (your listener). The best elevator speech will have the following three characteristics:

1. **Authentic** –Being authentic means speaking from the heart in a way that registers as true, honest and sincere.

Because the most captivating thing you can say is what you believe.

Finding your truth, and expressing it, is a central theme of the NEW Elevator Pitch. When you are at your most authentic, you are connected with your subject matter. You speak in a way that is your most natural and confident, avoiding the common speaker contortions that will keep your listener focused …on your fidgeting.

It's easy to come up with goofy one-liners, followed by a memorized list of features and benefits, but that's yesterday's news (or maybe, yesterday's mistakes. Those mistakes are best left in the past). It's time to stop pitching, and start connecting. Those real connections start with authentic communication.

Discussing your true convictions, in a way that seems unrehearsed and confident at the same time: THAT'S authenticity.

2. **Compelling** –Meaningful change is only meaningful if your message is compelling. Your words, your actions

and your gestures can mean the difference between a mess, and "YES!"

Nobody wants to give a pitch, just so that others can remain indifferent. There's enough noise online already. Make up your mind to create something that inspires. The NEW Elevator Pitch delivers a call to action. Are you clear about what you want, what you can deliver, and what you want your listener to do when you're done? Considering what you want others to do or say next is the key to developing your strongest possible elevator pitch. Aligning your capabilities with a compelling message is the power behind your communication.

3. **"Tell Me More..."** Judge the quality of your elevator pitch not by the quality of your diction, or your gestures, but on what people do when you are done. Focus your attention on what's most important: connecting with your audience.

When someone says, "Tell Me More..." that means that they are interested. It means that they clicked through to your blog. They read the report you referenced and watched that video; now it's time to provide your insight, in person. It's time for "Tell Me More..." Find out what your listener wants to know more about, and you have started the dialogue that is the foundation of the social space. Remember, no tweet or Facebook status tells your whole story. Neither does your elevator pitch. But it should be told in such a way that your listener takes the next logical step – moving from indifference, to action, by way of curiosity.

Authentic. Compelling. Tell me more... The characteristics of the NEW Elevator Pitch are easy to understand. Implementing those ideas can be easy as well, if you understand the process for your New Pitch.

What's in the Book?
This rest of this book is organized into two parts. The first part, *Pitch Perfect*, will teach you a seven-step technique for creating your NEW Elevator Pitch.

Every chapter in this section ends with an *Under Construction* exercise. These series of exercises will guide you through the process of perfecting your own pitch according to the seven-step process.

In an effort to address different "pitch" situations, the book also contains advice for speed networking, as well as guidelines for a variety of unexpected "elevator pitch" moments. By shattering some old conventions and disrupting traditional thinking, you can create a path to new mastery of your personal communication.

The best way to develop your pitch making skills is to practice. There really is no substitute for getting in front of the video camera, and taking a good long look at what you are delivering to the world. I know it can be tough to watch yourself, but if you don't know what you're doing right now, how can you ever improve?

It takes courage to put yourself on camera, and more courage to watch it afterwards. However, this step is key to making your message more powerful.

I believe that video is an important part of your learning, if you're serious about making a difference with your communication. So, I've included multiple quick-codes that will link you to videos that illustrate some of the finer points within the text. Simply use your smart phone to scan the code and you'll be taken to an important interactive message. There are other links to various online resources that I believe will create additional value for you.

In addition, I have included several brief exercises, designed to amplify the ideas in the particular chapter. These quick drills should be completed in two minutes or less.

Acceleration is important to me, and it is possible to get things done quickly if you know what you're doing. And, who doesn't have 118 seconds to improve their communication style? That's right. In just two minutes, you can make real progress, if you take the time to really engage for those two minutes. These drills are your accelerators – easy-to-handle exercises designed to help you inspire your listener, among other objectives. Here's the first one – take two minutes and respond honestly – and quickly!

2:00 All in the Timing

Before we start drilling into the differences between the old and new, we need to establish a baseline for your current elevator pitch. Choose one of the following questions; take two minutes to consider your response. Then, set the timer for two minutes – turn on the video camera or your smartphone - and deliver your response. Hit this QR code to see a video that will help you with creating an on-camera message that's straightforward and simple.

Shortlink: http://bit.ly/u0zb6v

Questions:

- Why don't you tell me a little bit about yourself?
- Why should I hire you?
- What exactly do you do for your job?
- Tell me a little bit about the company you represent.
- Regarding your education, what's been your most important learning experience, and why?

THE NEW ELEVATOR PITCH

How did you do? Rate yourself based on your time:

- **Over 2 minutes:** Do you need an editor?
- **1:45-2:00:** You've got something to say. Good work.
- **1:30-1:45:** Good start, but you need more material.
- **1:00-1:30:** Don't be shy, there's more to your story than you think.
- **Under 1:00:** Try again!

The upcoming chapters and exercises will help you with your timing, your material and your delivery. It's good to get used to putting your stories into a format of two minutes or less, because that's a perfect size – you can deliver key points, but it's not "War and Peace". When you completed the above exercise, were you surprised at how long two minutes can be?

The upcoming chapters will show you how to make your words work for you, while avoiding over-sharing, in a concentrated format. Timing is important but the real measurement of your success will be what your audience does with your story.

Putting Fun into the Fundamentals

What if you viewed your NEW Elevator Pitch as...fun? How would your delivery style change – could you give yourself permission to put "fun" into your fundamentals... and video your progress? You may find out that your fears (whatever they may be) are easily fixed with a quick change in your approach.

And we will talk about that change in detail; with the kind of instruction and examples you need to turn fear into fun. So, whether you are a college student, executive leader or superstar salesperson, I want to help you move the needle on your style and your substance. Everybody has room to improve – and not just improve your pitch, but improve your circumstances, with a persuasive message. You have the ability to make your message engaging and fun – if you allow yourself to do so...

(For more on how to turn the corner on your fear of public speaking, check out the resources on my website, http://www.pitchthefear.com)

2:00 Your Two-Minute Drill

In a recent survey, people listed "fear of public speaking" ahead of "fear of dying". These facts led Jerry Seinfeld to observe that the person delivering the eulogy at a funeral would probably rather be in the box, going into the ground, than delivering a speech in public. Do you feel the same way, when it's time to talk?

1. Take thirty seconds to recall your most painful public speaking experience. Ready? Begin.
2. Now, take ninety seconds or less to reflect on the outcome.

You survived. So what is there to be afraid of? What would you like to do differently, next time?

THE NEW ELEVATOR PITCH

Make a list of what you would like to change. Let's start your game plan for positive change, right now, with what you'd like to do differently in the future. Keep going – the future is just ahead...

Clarity is Crucial

OK. Before we dive into the first part of the book, let me introduce you to the Seven Steps to Stories that Stick. (I apologize in advance for the alliteration – whoops, I did it again!) The Seven Steps are the component parts of the NEW Elevator Pitch.

Consider a sentence or two that demonstrates each of the steps, and you will build your elevator pitch, with minimal effort. Then, use the two-minute drills to strengthen your skills. Later in the book, the Scenarios provide a platform for even more personal development. By the end of the book you will have more than just a pitch; you will have a method for being heard.

The Seven Steps to Stories that Stick is based on the foundation of all good communication: CLARITY.

The following chart describes CLARITY for the NEW Elevator Pitch:

C APTIVATE – step 1
L ANGUAGE of LEADERSHIP – step 2
A UTHENTICITY – step 3
R ELEVANCE – step 4
I NSPIRATION – step 5
T ACTFULNESS – step 6
Y ES – (NEXT STEPS) – step 7

YOUR HIGHLIGHT REEL

A Summary of the Key Ideas in this Chapter

The NEW Elevator Pitch should have three characteristics:

1. Authentic
2. Compelling
3. "Tell me more..."

Remember: Always deliver your pitch with CLARITY- the seven steps to stories that stick

You have made it through speechmaking in the past; you are taking steps to change your presentation skills, and your belief system, through the NEW Elevator Pitch. You've survived; now it's time to thrive.

So, are you ready to get started, with captivating your audience?

UNDER CONSTRUCTION

As you read through the book, I will show you how to craft your own NEW Elevator Pitch. Each step of the process will be marked "Under Construction".

So what does a NEW Elevator Pitch look like? Here's a quick sketch – picture this:

Fifteen sentences, 160 words, and it takes less than two minutes to deliver. That's all you need for a NEW Elevator Pitch. Maybe you have more words, or maybe less. Timing is important, but being concise is crucial. Don't overthink it, and don't over-tell it. Choose the words that help you most; leave the rest behind.

We'll start writing your pitch at the end of the next chapter. By the end of this book, you will have in your hand a convincing, well written elevator pitch, the first of many you will be making throughout the rest of your career. So get your paper and pencil ready and write down your answer to the following question.

What is the focus of your first NEW Elevator Pitch?
Here are some possibilities:

- Getting a job
- Getting a raise
- Getting a date
- Expanding your network
- Communicating with your coworkers

- Creating social change
- Inspiring a movement
- Gaining an investor

Got your theme? Let's keep going!

Part I

The Seven Steps to Clarity

Captivate

"There is no such thing as an attention span. People have infinite attention if you are entertaining them." – *Jerry Seinfeld*

"I don't have a short attention span, I just...Oh, look! A Kitty!" – *Anonymous*

"The first eight seconds is the length of time the average human can concentrate on something and not lose some focus." – *Jeffrey Hayzlett,* The Mirror Test

So, Tell Me A Little Bit About Yourself...

There it is, that deceptive softball question that brings out your most common elevator pitch. The number one issue that keeps people from delivering a strong response is the lack of a strong opening. You must gain the attention of your listener, or what follows won't really matter. You have to CAPTIVATE your audience.

PART I: SEVEN STEPS TO CLARITY

Get Their Attention

Let's face it, you gotta get their attention. Maybe your listener is thinking about a kitty, or Jeffrey Hayzlett, or about how you are not as funny as Jerry Seinfeld. The NEW Elevator Pitch lives and dies on your opening, so it's got to be a good one. But remember our criteria from before: the best elevator speech is authentic, compelling and relevant (it makes someone say, "Tell Me More..."). While your intro needs to grab someone's attention, it's even more critical that it inspires action. The action you want to inspire with your opening is rapt attention. You want your audience to say, "Tell me more..." What's the secret to being captivating? The answer is right in front of you. You have to understand your audience.

Start With Your Audience

The strongest opening is the one that has the most direct appeal to your listener. As you probably already know, everyone is running a mental software program that makes them ask, "What's in it for me?" and then, right after that, "Why should I care?" (I assume that you already know that about this aspect of human nature, because those are the questions you are probably asking yourself right now as you read this book).

The first thing that you must do to capture your listener is to know who they are, and what they are about.

The best openers start with recognition of the person that's right in front of your face. If you really know your story, you can start with theirs – that's the secret to captivating your audience.

1. Who is your audience? Take them in, and acknowledge what's going on around you.
2. What do you think your audience is thinking right now? What's their number one concern? START THERE.
3. Create an opening that represents who you are, in a way that is unexpected or disarming. Don't be afraid to be unpredictable – that can be very interesting, BUT:

Don't dive into some goofy cliché or tough-to-follow metaphor. What are you about, and where are you headed, and why do you need verbal "Jazz-hands" to make your point? Leave the gimmicks behind.

Your Audience IS Your Subject
Consider your opening in general terms that can be broadly appealing to your audience– and supported by specifics in the remainder of your elevator pitch.

Recognition
What is it that occupies your listener's mind: is it cost-cutting? Revenue generation? Inventory levels? Going out to dinner on Saturday with someone new? Funding initiatives in cancer research? To captivate your audience, you need to present a solution that is not just on their mind, but 'top-of-mind'.

PART I: SEVEN STEPS TO CLARITY

Recognition is the first step in captivating your audience. You have to really see the person in front of you. Seeing someone, really seeing them, is not a science experiment or an awkward drawn out process, to acknowledge what you already know. Connection happens naturally, all the time, when we meet with others. Think back to a conversation where you delivered (or could have delivered) a persuasive conversation. What exactly was happening with your listener, just before the conversation started?

Thinking about the "who" in front of you doesn't have to be an elaborate process. Remember that person that you saw at breakfast, or your friend that you met for lunch yesterday. What was their mood? How did they seem to be doing? Rarely does anyone answer, "I have no idea!"

Each of us has the ability to reflect and consider the person (or people) we are speaking to – yet we rarely use it. While some have higher abilities to empathize than others (also called an "EQ" or emotional intelligence), we all have the ability to recognize our surroundings. My question for you is: how often do you use your "super-powers" of human perception? Do you take a moment to consider the "who" in a way that evaluates their moods, their interests, and their concerns? (Those moments are free, by the way, so take as many as you need!)

Awareness

What's typically missing from a great opening statement is our awareness of our surroundings, or our circumstances. Connect with your audience by showing your connection to the current state of affairs, the current status of your listener, and your current understanding of what's happening right now.

Plug in with your surroundings and your audience will plug in with you. Acknowledge what's going on, or what's gone on, to establish candor and honesty for your listener.

2:00 Your Two-Minute Drill

Acknowledge Your Surroundings, in two minutes or less:

Look around you right now. Are you on a plane? In an office? In your living room? Find a way to notice and comment on your surroundings that's POSITIVE and reinforces your pitch.

1. Just start with a stream of consciousness, "The fan is blowing. Lisa is looking for something in her desk, I can hear her rummaging. The sun is setting, it will be night time soon..." Write down five observations.

2. Take your observations and put them in service, in opening your pitch. Choose one, or combine a couple for your opener.

Examples:

- "Listening to that air conditioner always reminds me how we have to keep our cool, when it comes to the competition. If you've seen the latest edition of that trade magazine, you know what I'm talking about..."

- "Our customers are searching for us online, and they can't find what they're looking for unless we use video more effectively. I mean, YouTube is the #2 search engine, so why are we fumbling around in the dark when we could easily put a video online, right now?"

Practice using your perceptions, and put 'em to work for you – it only takes a couple of minutes!

We are all dominated by other thoughts, issues, concerns and a self-absorbed nature ("What's in it for me?" is universal). "I'm meeting you...but I'm thinking about me" is the inner dialogue for many. That self-centered focus causes us to rarely reflect on what we all see and hear. Yet, everyone is wired to observe and report – we can always tune in to other folks, if we choose to.

Framing

I learned a difficult lesson about the importance of framing the conversation, especially when you are meeting someone for the first time. Here's what happened on my first meeting with a coaching client from the pharmaceutical industry:

"Chris," she said to me, "I've heard so many good things about you from my friend that referred me. Why don't you tell me a little bit about yourself?"

Aha, I thought to myself, THIS is going to be easy! Filled with flattery and full of pride, I considered my answer. I've got this one!

"Well, I'm the national elevator pitch champion," I said with a smile.

"That's' great!" she said. "What's an elevator pitch?"

Most of the time we are so focused on what's next that we forget about who's here. Framing the conversation can be helpful to set the stage for your listener, with introductory phrases like these:

Have you noticed...?

You know how...?

I'll never forget the time when....

Doesn't it seem like...?

These establishing statements can set up your topic, and are particularly useful when:

You are involved in speed networking or other formalized networking events

When meeting people from a variety of backgrounds and interests, or meeting someone whose background and interests are uncertain

You need to establish a persuasive topic that is perhaps unexpected or unusual for your audience (they need a frame of reference)

You are meeting someone for the first time, and you need to get them thinking with you on your topic or agenda.

 *Shortlink:*   *http://bit.ly/wq9vlr*

The next two-minute drill shows you how to incorporate your perceptions and frame your pitch around your listener. Notice how these examples link "right now" to what's next, as part of a powerful opening. Can you guess the audience, and the circumstances?

2:00 Your Two-Minute Drill

Review these Examples of captivating opening remarks and answer the questions below in less than two minutes. First, the opening remarks.

"When it comes time to lead a team, I'm looking for people who understand customer service on a personal level. If you've had a bad customer experience, and you want to make sure that something like that never happens to your client, I want to talk to you..."

"Getting into the MBA program here at Duke was an important accomplishment for me, but not nearly as important as the lesson I learned last Christmas in Afghanistan. Let me explain what I mean..."

"When I was working for Sun, the one thing I realized was how important software is to the life-blood of the business. What happens if your capacity just isn't enough for the company – and customers think your technology has just 'run out'?"

Questions:
1. Who do you suppose is the audience for each of these presentations?
2. How does each one take in the circumstances, or the listener, with a disarming comment?
3. How would these pitches make you say, "Tell Me More..." – tell me more about what, exactly?

Adaptability

In addition to core concerns and surrounding, you have to consider your audience's style: Are you speaking to someone who is gregarious, and outgoing? Perhaps you need to ramp up your energy and your volume to match theirs; otherwise your pitch will be dismissed as noise. If you are talking with folks who are standing at a cocktail party, laughing and discussing things in an animated way, and you shift into a rehearsed robotic speech, you will not only kill the mood, you will never be heard. Similarly, chatting with highly-analytical folks, or a more reserved crowd, may not be the place for power-pacing and bold gesture patterns. As you tailor your remarks to your listener, consider too your personal presentation style.

Most of us have a particular presentation style that represents our comfort zone. I can seem bold and gregarious to some, but it's not exactly my nature. Similarly, I can illustrate facts with figures, and provide the kind of analysis that supports particular principles. Actually, that doesn't feel like my wheelhouse, either. But what is a strength of mine is *reading* the audience – knowing *who* is the first step to discussing *what*. Adaptability is the key to that initial connection.

Even when you are the boss and you are laying out the plans, success is all about your approach. Most organizations operate, on some level, as a benevolent dictatorship. The buck has to stop somewhere, and not all conversations are going to be brought up for a vote.

Some elevator speeches end with someone very upset, unhappy, or unemployed. Build a platform of respect and acknowledgement no matter what your message. Without a foundation of personal respect, your desired results are hard to grasp. Good news or bad: the new elevator speech is a powerful tool, and it deserves a powerful introduction.

When you are the person in charge, it's even more critically important for you to approach your employees, your team or your constituents in a way that prepares them to engage with your ideas. Choose the path that gets you to the results you want; if a hard-driving style is all you've got, maybe you should consider some coaching. Your words are vitally important to your team; choose them carefully.

- "Times are tough, and we've got more cuts in front of us. Unless... and this is a big 'unless'...unless we can increase operational efficiency by 12% in the next quarter."

- "There is a way to make it through this; we just have to work together on the plan."

- "Sacrifices are going to have to be made. We will see if we really understand the difference between discipline and regret, my friends."

- "People have been underestimating us for a long time, especially our competition. Today, the announcement of our new distribution is going to change the game.

PART I: SEVEN STEPS TO CLARITY

We will have more shelf space than ever before, but it's still not enough. I need your help...."

The Match Game

On the next page, there are some possible scenarios that you may find warrant an elevator speech. You may be asked to introduce yourself, or to deliver a message regarding a particular idea or initiative. All elevator speeches are persuasive, so matching energy is the first step towards persuading your listener to engage with you.

Let's consider some of these audience descriptions and how you can address their concerns and their energy in a way that gets your message heard and understood:

Crowd that's Laughing, High-energy:

You have to match the energy and use appropriate gestures, picking up on the cues around you. Otherwise, your story won't be heard. Similarly, don't be a "Debbie Downer" – even if you have important bad news, consider the timing and move slowly towards that message. Timing is everything: Is this the right time for your pitch? Is this the right crowd?

The Boss Has Some 'Closed-Off" Body Language

Build into your pitch with a disarming opening; something on-topic but unexpected: "I can see your frustration, but the answer could be less than two minutes away." If that last statement feels like a stretch or a gimmick, go back to noticing your surroundings: "I don't want to presume, but you seem [INSERT EMOTION HERE]" "The solution could be right in front of us, we just haven't been able to identify it. I was speaking to Cathy in the warehouse..." Your solution is your leading statement here.

Meeting with Analyticals: Scientists, Finance Professionals, Engineers, etc.

If you are a member of such a group, your style is probably ideally suited. However, social butterflies and gregarious, non-linear expressives will need to take it down a notch (or 12). What energy and pacing (the speed of your speech, not walking around) would serve you best in reaching this group? You have the ability to choose; you operate on more than instinct. Observe and notice those around you - adjust your delivery level for your audience. You don't change who you are to suit the audience – you simply consider a style adjustment that fits the room (and the people in it).

To captivate someone's attention, you have to first place yours on them. Knowing your story is important, but knowing your audience is what really matters. You have to "take in" your listener: Are they agitated? Concerned? Closed off to new ideas? You better find out, if you want to captivate their imagination for the next two minutes.

PART I: SEVEN STEPS TO CLARITY

Create an Opening

The new elevator speech often starts in a way that is unexpected, sometimes disarming. And sometimes you have to start with an assumption about your audience. What's the solution you can provide? What can you do for your audience – or, with their help?

Good openers come from a place that says, "I recognize you. I recognize your concerns. I am a solutions provider that could have exactly what you need."

Notice the words "could have". Be careful about coming in too strong. "I've got all the answers" is not captivating, because no one really does. You have promoted yourself to a suspicious status, if you claim too much too soon. "I know what you need" is a bold statement, the verbal equivalent of kicking down the door. Even if you do have what someone needs, please knock first.

If you have a solution, prepare us to listen. It's not your job to judge the validity of your remarks ("they're great" or "they stink" are both wrong, and it's not your place to choose). Concentrate instead on captivating your audience, not intimidating them. You have to focus on the delivery and on grabbing your audience's attention. If you've got all the answers, your listener immediately thinks, "Why do you need me?" and then, "Why do I need to listen to you?" as they await your orders. Instantly, you've lost your audience. Any intro that's a version of "Here's my way, there's the highway" is a total turn off.

And remember to keep it brief. "I believe that my 43-page treatise on the budgetary comparisons for the next five years, based on last week's pro forma as modified by the finance department at our West Campus..." Wow. You lost me before the first quotation mark.

Opening Orders

Here are some more tips that can help you avoid common pitfalls and mistakes in your opening statements.

Don't Delay

Acknowledge your surroundings, but move on quickly. Don't open with something that would indicate a lack of focus; concentrate on your audience and make sure that you have them from the start.

"You know how, when you're standing at the checkout line at the Von's, or maybe the Ralph's, and there are all these magazines and I can't help but wondering what the latest and greatest insignificant details of..." Blah blah blah. Extra negative credit for staying focused on yourself, never making a point, and touring the weeds for your audience. Establish, and GO! The NEW Elevator Pitch is about what matters and you MUST focus on your listener. Acknowledge your surroundings, and connect with your audience.

Remember: 8 seconds is all you've got, so start strong!

Shortlink: http://bit.ly/jZvkju

Don't Rush Toward the Ending

Your objective is to captivate – but don't "sell the wine before it's time". Business is a process, and your communication needs to follow a pattern – so that others can follow along, and you earn the right to advance on your message. While Steven Covey says we should "Begin with the end in mind," that doesn't mean that you blurt it out in your opening remarks.

Your audience needs a few seconds to engage, and for you to check in and see if you've got their attention.

Don't Apologize

Have you heard (or used) a variation of this one:

"I'm sorry about the copier/slide projector/ haircut/humidity/traffic in Connecticut/news release/weather/will of God/things beyond my control/outside world."

Please stop any apology that is unnecessary. As Katherine Hepburn famously said, "Don't complain, don't explain." Many times I've heard presenters use the apologetic opener, and it makes me want to rush the podium with a roll of duct tape. However, when you give as many presentations as I have, you make your own share of mistakes. I've opened with an unnecessary apology too, but the "I'm sorry" opening is something I had to cut out of my vocabulary.

Think about it: Do you want people to feel sorry for you? You may feel like you are being accommodating or polite, but more likely you are coming off as unfocused. Best to leave apologies aside as best you can.

"Sorry" starters are purely a distraction, and your listener interprets it as:

- A stalling tactic.
- A propped-up delay for a disconnected speaker
- Permission not to pay attention, cause you haven't gotten anywhere near what really matters
- Asking for pity, a feeble attempt to connect with an audience on the weakest possible level

Yikes! That's the exact opposite of what you want in the NEW Elevator Pitch. You want to captivate your listener, not confound them! There's too much noise already, people are already posting pictures of their breakfast on Facebook, or complaining about their kids.

PART I: SEVEN STEPS TO CLARITY

The NEW Elevator Pitch is the place where you have to get to the important stuff – No Apologies Necessary.

Sometimes you have to explain certain things about your environment, when a mic doesn't work or the room is hot because the air conditioning is broken. Don't barrel into your pitch until you've set aside whatever environmental concerns, issues or apologies you really need to offer. But, ESPECIALLY if you are in front of a group: don't say something just to appear service-minded! Your story is your best service.

Create a compelling vision: When I talk to graduate students, my opening remarks (no matter the presentation) are about the future. Want to know why? Because it's the number one thing on every graduate's mind.

Do you remember your graduation? Everyone is there, offering you congratulations, but all you can think about is, "Now what?" For me, in many of my college presentations, I use a variation of this basic introduction: "Everybody talks about the past, everybody talks about current events, but my focus is on the future. And not just any future, but your future…"

Shortlink: http://bit.ly/yIFv79

Captivating? Interesting? Does it make you say, "Tell me more…?" A great platform for your introduction is a new vision of what things might look like, for those who engage with your elevator pitch. Create a compelling vision, and you will truly captivate your audience from word #1.

Some common questions:

1. **But what if my opening is too general?** There's no such thing. Consider my example from talking to college crowds: There is nothing more general than the future. The future is unknown and uncertain – that's precisely why we are all concerned about it! Specifics will come, but you want to be general enough to give yourself the opportunity to elaborate. Remember, your objective is "Tell me more…" so don't try to tell me everything – you can't do it in an elevator pitch. Create an opening that states something that is universal – something that we can all identify – if you want to

create a connection. The specifics will come, but start off with something that makes your audience say, "Yeah… I know what you mean!"

2. **Sometimes I don't know my audience.** When you are meeting with a group, especially in an informal setting, it's hard to know who's who in the zoo. Is she the CFO, or the marketing director, or your boss's wife? Your pitch should vary, depending on the audience, but who's who? What about a "why hire me?" pitch – don't you know the "who" before you move to the "why"? In a word, no. You have to make assumptions about what the company needs. Concentrate on the solution that you provide, the difference that you make, the service you can illuminate for your audience. If you are a surgeon and the company needs a plumber, why are you pitching, anyway? Assume that you are the solution – or, find another elevator!

   Dicey Dialogue: Then there's the scenario where your best elevator pitch for an executive audience could totally terrify a group of employees (that's usually true for consultants or outsourced IT professionals – what if you have information about the upcoming layoffs, or the performance rankings of the entire customer service department?) How do you tell the VIP (very important person) from the NBD (no big deal)? First of all, treat everyone with respect and consideration. That VIP was once NBD, FYI.

STEP 1: CAPTIVATE

Here's how to beat the unknown audience issue:

Ask your listener to clarify their role or their concern with a specific question. "Are you more focused on R&D, or product development, right now?" "Does that initiative for new markets apply to your department?" Get the listener to tell you more, so that you make your message as powerful as possible. "Fools rush in", the saying goes, so make sure you know what's on your audience's mind before you plow forward. That's also the case if you are giving a more formal presentation, or touching base with a large group. Make contact with people before you speak; talk with them and find out what's on their minds. You owe it to yourself and to your audience to start where they are, so they can get to where you need them to be.

I just know that they are not with me! – That can be a sinking feeling, when you start off with what you think is a bang, but it lands with a thud. How do you recover, when your best opener fails to captivate? The best advice is to remember your focus. You're not done; you've still got an opportunity to captivate with the rest of your speech. Some folks are slow to connect, don't let that stop you from trying. Your message is important enough for you to push onward, and make sure that your energy, tone and pace are right on track.

PART I: SEVEN STEPS TO CLARITY

Shortlink: http://bit.ly/yMIDz5

One of my favorite stories about Johnny Carson, the former host of the "Tonight Show" was about what he whispered to himself during the monologue. (Now, I'm not sure if he really whispered to himself, and I can't confirm where I heard this story – it could be an urban legend, for all I know - but it always stuck with me. So consider this an inside story, or just a parable – whatever suits you).

When the audience seemed a little off, or the jokes weren't quite on track, Carson would remind himself, "Stick to the script. Stick to the script." It's easy to lose faith in your material, and want to improvise, especially if an elevator pitch represents new territory for you. But what you've worked on is still your best material, even if it looks like you might bomb. That's not to say that there won't be variety in your delivery, and in your material. But consider that what you've prepared is going to be stronger than what you've just thought up, unless you are someone like Robin Williams (notorious for never following a script, especially during his early days in television).

STEP 1: CAPTIVATE

Sometimes the NEW Elevator Pitch is an exercise in improvisation; but if you've rehearsed your key points, make sure you make them. Deliver the story that you have prepared, and say it with energy and confidence. Your best story is the one you have considered; don't leave your preparation behind if you don't get the initial reaction you had hoped for.

The objective is "Tell me More..." but sometimes your audience has heard enough, before you even start. Don't get discouraged – keep moving, keep telling your story, and keep working towards a positive, active result. All you can control is what you have to say, and how you say it. Work towards the action you want, with a powerful opening. Be engaged, and engaging, with a high-energy statement that captivates, and you are on your way to your best elevator pitch ever.

Name, Rank, and Job Description

What about some more examples of powerful openings, for your elevator speech:

• "Turning around companies sounds pretty general, but that's where we get specific – it starts with connecting with the people and plugging in with the operations of your business. My name is Mike Ramos and my company..."

- "You seem frustrated, and I can understand why. But the answer to your concerns could be less than two minutes away."

- "Teamwork is something that we need to talk about. Let's face it; none of us is as smart as all of us. I'm Linda McCallum, and as a facilitator, I help organizations..."

- "I can't fix the state of our industry, but I want to share with you a three-step process that will help us face next year with new resources and funding."

- "Why can't small colleges attract major employers, for job interviews? If you'll give me two minutes, I can show you how we can bring the mountain to Mohammed..."

- "My title says that I run the marketing department, but my real strength is in managing our media relationships. My name is...."

- "Most people know me from my last screenplay. But my focus here at the Gottlieb Cancer Center is on telling your story, and creating a reason for greater donations for the children's wing...."

Notice that none of these start with, "My name is Barry, and I'm a [INSERT JOB DESCRIPTION OR TITLE HERE]." Who you are and what you do are important, but not as important as what you can do for others. Promise yourself to go beyond a simple introduction; your objective is to CAPTIVATE.

Your audience may be curious about you, but they're thinking about themselves. Everybody in the Beginner's Class starts their elevator pitch with their name and job description (Yawn). Why do that? Why not accelerate your conversations with a powerful introduction, which shows that you are in tune with your listener?

The solutions you provide and the problems you can solve are more captivating – more interesting – than your name, rank and serial number. Don't expect your title to command respect – offer a solution and earn the right to tell your story. Acknowledge your listener, and begin with a surprising and honest remark about who you are – that's the most captivating story you can tell.

`2:00` Your Two-Minute Drill

Develop three powerful opening statements. You have 120 seconds, so set the timer and go. Time is of the essence – don't over-think your elevator pitch. Three statements, two minutes: don't wait till Christmas to come up with your answer!

If you are working with friends, a coach, or a group, consider the opening statement that is most appropriate for your listener(s). Your opener should make the listener want to know more.

Will you start your elevator speech with a question? Why or why not? Sometimes a question can be a great opener. After you complete your Two-Minute Drill, ask for feedback: Which opener did you like best, and why? Remember, it will never be your best pitch until someone else has heard it.

YOUR HIGHLIGHT REEL
A Summary of the Key Ideas in this Chapter

- Recognize your audience, and your surroundings
- Move quickly to the solution you can provide, or the outcome you'd like to discuss
- Match your energy to the group, and don't apologize
- Say your name and title if (and when) it makes sense – AFTER you connect with your audience

UNDER CONSTRUCTION
CLARITY: Step 1 is Captivate

Seven steps to tell your story. Do you realize that you can create one or two sentences for each of the steps, and build a speech that will take about two minutes? Of course, it depends on how you write, and how fast you speak, but 14-18 good sentences will take you approximately 2:00.

At the end of each chapter, you'll see the "Under Construction"– it's a gentle reminder to put your work down on you "Pitch Paper" – the sheet where you build your pitch, one sentence at a time.

Example of a pitch paper:

Pitch Paper
Speak with CLARITY

CAPTIVATE
LANGUAGE
AUTHENTICITY
RELEVANCE
INSPIRATION
TACT
YES!
Tell Me More…   About….
               1.
               2.
               3.

Dowload the pitch paper:

Shortlink: http://bit.ly/pitchpaper

How easy is that?

CAPTIVATE is the first step. Start your Pitch Paper, with an opening that captivates. Write it down, and save it till you finish the next chapter.

Language

"It's a strange world of language in which skating on thin ice can get you into hot water."
– *Franklin P. Jones*

"The very essence of leadership is you have a vision. It's got to be a vision you articulate clearly and forcefully ..."
– *Theodore Hesburgh, President Emeritus of the University of Notre Dame*

"Our major obligation is not to mistake slogans for solutions." – *Edward R. Murrow, American broadcast journalist*

Congratulations, you've captivated your audience.

Now they want to know where you're going. It's time for you to lay out your thoughts and ideas in a way that your audience can comprehend. In other words, What type of language are you going to use?

PART I: SEVEN STEPS TO CLARITY

Common conversations can create uncommon results, when you present with passion and conviction. And language is the key to outlining what you can do with, through and for others.

Language Arts

Language is important at every level. Language is key to explaining your themes and ideas. The words you chose will define who you are and how your message is received.

Using the proper language, you have the opportunity to lead your listener to a new conclusion. You have the opportunity to help others to see a different outcome – an outcome where your project gets funded, your product gets bought, your position becomes available or your screenplay gets produced.

So many times, our first efforts fall flat in the old elevator pitch – our language isn't strong enough to make our point. Don't blow an uncertain trumpet, as Theodore Hesburgh says – use the words that will cut through the noise.

Consider the elevator speech of my friend, Fred, whose opener was:

"I'm the Joe Montana of marketing…."

While I love and respect Joe Montana, the first thing that went through my head was that Fred must be a retired champion – or someone who enjoyed wearing Skechers. (As I write this, Mr. Montana is the spokesperson for the brand. And a hall-of-fame quarterback. What's the connection?)

Maybe Fred was trying to convey that he was a clutch player, a go-to-MVP kind of guy, just like Joe Montana. But he used the wrong language. His metaphor was mixed, and I got lost in the interpretation. His story was gone in 16 seconds.

You don't want to spend your elevator pitch explaining your opening remarks. Some comparisons may be polarizing, confusing, or both:

- "I'm the Donald Trump of the local plumbing market"
- "I'm the Rudy Ruettiger of the shipping department"
- "I'm the 'Green Lantern' of strategic marketing"

What were your responses, on a gut level, to those openers? The Trumpster is a polarizing figure. Rudy Ruettiger – do you recognize that name? He is the former Notre Dame player who represents one of the greatest underdog stories of all time – featured in the movie, "Rudy" starring Sean Astin. And, Green Lantern? Well, what the heck does that comparison even mean?

PART I: SEVEN STEPS TO CLARITY

Sometimes opening with a metaphor can be a great way to grab someone's attention, if you know they have a common frame of reference. But how can you be sure that this is the right language to use for your audience? If you are talking with people inside your company, or industry, a common denominator could be a good choice...or it could be just common. Is there a stronger (broader) choice out there for you? Seek language that is general enough to be interesting, and specific enough to inspire others to say, "Tell me more..."

Your opening should not be cryptic; you are speaking with CLARITY, after all. Don't find some obscure metaphor that defies your listener's logic and understanding. If someone needs Wikipedia or ESPN to grasp your opening line, better head back to the drawing board.

Similarly, watch out for clichés or catch-phrases. You're not trying to come up with a skit for *Saturday Night Live*.

The Subject at Hand

After your introduction captivates your listener, it's time to lay out your subject. What is it that you want people to understand? Understanding takes many shapes: there's listening ("I understand what you're saying") there's the emotional connection ("Wow. After that presentation, I really believe in what the Alley Theater means to Houston!") and then there's understanding that leads to agreement ("I hear what you're saying, and it's the right thing to do. Let's move forward with your recommendation") Above all else, the language you use must cause the audience to respond by saying, "Tell me more…"

Consider moving quickly and powerfully to your key theme, with the kind of language that lets your listener know what's expected. In this Two-Minute Drill, you can do just that – take two minutes to isolate the driving force behind your pitch.

2:00 Your Two-Minute Drill

Quickly answer these questions about your NEW Elevator Pitch in two minutes or less. Ready?

- What do you want others to do, when your message is done?
- What are your recommendations for your audience, or for the company, the patient, the team, or the students?
- What is your theme – the initial 'discovery' that makes people say, "Tell me more…"?

What language can you use to create the interest you established in your opening remarks?

The Language of Leadership

When you are presenting to a group, or to an important individual, you are an expert on your subject. Like it or not, you are in a position of leadership – even if it's just thought leadership – and you have the floor. Your audience wants to know your vision. Have you got one?

How do you express your vision? That's the language of leadership.

Shortlink: http://youtu.be/dxzRw82mwG4

On a grand scale, your vision may be for a huge social initiative, like fighting a life-threatening disease, feeding the poor, establishing a new foundation, or improving our school systems. But what about vision on a smaller scale – a day-to-day kind of vision that influences the people around us towards that "thing that they cannot provide for themselves"?

My friend Kelly O'Brien is the Director for the Center for Productive Communication at Texas Christian University – consistently rated as one of the top MBA programs in the US for developing strong business communication skills. Early in his career, Kelly was making a presentation and a senior associate asked, "What do you recommend that we do, Kelly?" Humbly, Kelly offered an idea, and said, "...if you think that makes sense." His colleague shot back, "How do I know if it makes sense? You've done the research. You know this material. YOU ARE THE EXPERT. If you feel strongly about it, just say so and let's move forward." Kelly did exactly that: he gave himself permission to be the expert. Kelly realized that he had to use the language of leadership to make his NEW Elevator Pitch work.

Leadership and Vision

Leadership plays a part in developing the language of your pitch. You must lead with language; provide the words and the vision that others can follow. Maybe it's an understanding of the current budget, with recommendations for spending reductions next year – is this topic significant enough for some leadership insight? I say yes! In fact, your story is lost without language. Perhaps it's a diagnosis and treatment plan that can make a difference in someone's recovery from a wrist injury. Does leadership play a role here? The patient who is looking for guidance would say "yes" – please choose the words that can help me most! Language always matters. An executive conversation with several board members always touches on the future, for a multi-billion dollar company. Come to think of it, what persuasive conversation doesn't require the language of leadership? Powerful language is the only choice for you. Articulate your vision for change, no matter the size of your objective.

PART I: SEVEN STEPS TO CLARITY

For the purpose of the NEW Elevator Pitch, your vision is the change that you would like to see happen. Your vision is your view of the status quo, and how you'd like it to change (we'll get to 'why' in upcoming chapters). All elevator pitches are persuasive, so what result would you like to persuade others to accomplish? Even if your topic is something mundane, like the advertising plan for next quarter, or the new booth design for the trade show, consider what these things might mean to your audience. Consider how you could use language to create opportunity.

See how using different language can dramatically change the impact of your vision in the NEW Elevator Pitch.

Lead-Off Language:
Same Message, Different Connection

Boring:
> "The new trade show booth is going to be 20' x 30', with a drop-down banner that can be seen from the entrance to the convention center. Traffic is supposed to be up by 14% this year. I think we're probably going to need more staff support at the show."

VS.

Scoring:
> "We've increased our booth space by 25% this year, with a banner that will be visible to 100% of

participants as they enter the show– that's why we are going to need more staff support this year. Here are some ideas on how you can help…"

Boring:

"The purpose of my elevator pitch is to convince you that the advertising budget should be increased in Q4. The holiday season could be an important time for us, and we should do what we can to support the end-of-year retail push."

VS.

Scoring:

"There's an opportunity for us at the end of the year. If we invest in additional advertising for the holidays, we could see a spike in Q4 revenues. Based on the plan I've outlined, a small investment is our fastest way to an end-of-year bonus for everybody…"

OLD NEWS VS. NEW IDEAS

Details on what it all means VS.

Details on what it all means to YOU

Features and Benefits VS.

Clear Opportunities for YOU

Numbers VS.

Impact of the Numbers

What we've done VS.
Where we are going

Which message focuses on your listener, and makes your audience say, "Tell me more..."?

Even if you don't see yourself as a leader, others may. Did you know that? People are looking to you for your guidance – your vision – in your elevator speech. People want to know who you are and what you can offer, as well as what skills or observations you bring to the conversation.

2:00 Your Two-Minute Drill

In two minutes or less, choose some powerful words that would strengthen your story for the following audiences.

- Engineers
- Sales people
- Sorority sisters
- A team of fifth grade boys
- The hiring manager for the new job you want
- A key audience of your own choosing

Did you alter your language for each of these audiences? If not, why not?

Pitching Up

It's tricky to use the language of leadership when you are talking to someone who may be above you in the hierarchy. Using the proper language is essential here to get the proper message delivered properly to an influential decision maker.

For many, the elevator speech is an opportunity to make an introduction for a new position – a job offer is the desired ultimate result. But, after a captivating introduction, it may seem both premature (and immature) to say something like, "I've discovered that, based on your job description and my personal skill set, that I'm the perfect candidate for the role. Here's how I know I'm the best..."

While that may be your ideal outcome, that's not the ideal approach. Stating your endgame before you've proven the merits is called an inappropriate judgment. It's inappropriate to project a decision onto your listener, especially before you've supported it. The key to getting your message across without alienating your listener is to use the right language.

Statements to Avoid Inappropriate Judgments:

- I believe...
- It seems that you...
- Would you agree that...?

Followed by a request for confirmation: "Do you agree?" "Did I get that right?"

Don't Force the Issue

The objective is for your listener to say, "Tell me more..." not "I submit to your will!" The NEW Elevator Pitch is about inspiring change; compliance is not enough, so don't drive towards it. Leading people to the right conclusion doesn't mean forcing something down their throats. Even if you are delivering a difficult message with only one possible outcome and you are explaining how things are going to unfold, you have to focus on your part of the conversation – interpreting "you" isn't up to you. Your mission, should you choose to accept it, is to lead your listeners to your desired outcome; otherwise you won't create lasting change. Your elevator pitch is a persuasive business case, not a blurt-fest. Steven Covey says to "begin with the end in mind," but that doesn't mean you blast your audience with your endgame and wait for their agreement. You have to earn the right to advance, with your elevator pitch.

Earning the Right to Advance

Earning the right to advance means building trust and agreement. Earning the right to advance means that you will not ask a question before its time. Sometimes you have theories and ideas that need to be tested; however, an unsupported judgment call is not persuasive; you don't earn the right to advance.

Asserting something before you've earned the right to advance can be disastrous.

Making an incorrect assumption can stall your elevator speech at the first floor. Asking questions to confirm can get your elevator back in motion. Questions are vitally important. Sometimes the questions you ask are even more important than the information you deliver. Don't get locked in to yesterday's idea that a pitch is a monologue. If you're not interacting with your listener, you're never going to win. Remember, the NEW Elevator Pitch is a way to start the dialogue. So, don't be afraid to get the conversation started!

In a job interview, you will undoubtedly be asked a variation on these two questions:

"Why don't you tell me a little bit about yourself?"

"Why should I hire you?"

At a basic instinct level, your response may be: "Hire me: Because I'm the best! Because I want it the most! Because I'm really, really desperate! What more do you need to know about me?"

Perhaps there is a better approach. Earning the right to advance means becoming a solutions provider. By shifting your mindset to providing solutions, you can answer the following questions – the universal questions that must be clarified before anyone gets hired to do anything:

What is the solution you provide? What problems can you resolve for your potential employer? How would your potential employer be better off with you on board? Instead of focusing on your accomplishments, put your attention on how your accomplishments can make a difference for the hiring manager, or the Board of Directors.

Remember, the NEW Elevator Pitch can be (and should be!) a dialogue with your audience. Check in, and find out if you're on the right track.

If you have earned the right to advance, what's the next logical step? Your final goal may be to sell the story, win the job, get the girl, or whatever else inspires you. But earning the right to advance is the strategy: don't get ahead of yourself.

To find out more about some powerful advice for your job search, visit my website: http://www.jobresourceacademy.com or just capture the QR code on the previous page.

2:00 Your Two-Minute Drill

If you wish to influence and persuade, you have to tap into your "inner leader" and share that quality with your audience. All elevator pitches are persuasive, and leadership unlocks the door to your key theme, or message. Have you got one yet?

Write out one theme three different ways (if you feel certain about your subject).

Examples:
1. I really need the team to get behind the new purchasing software.
2. The new purchasing software is going to make a difference for the company, if we let it.
3. Getting on board with the new software means your job will be much, much easier – but there are some changes that have to be made.

The most compelling way to phrase your theme is always:

• In terms of your audience: their wants, needs and concerns
• Your desired outcome: your wants, needs and concerns

- Unifying those two viewpoints, based on a beneficial outcome for your listener, your team or your business

---

- How does your desired outcome help your listener?
- Considering the topic of your elevator pitch, what's the main thing on your listener's mind?
- What is your listener's greatest concern, or fear, and how can you help them to address that issue?

Winning Themes

- Establish the funding for your initiative
- Gain agreement around the new proposal
- Allow the family to make a decision about their child's health

Body Language

Our times are very informal, and our online communication sometimes borders on incomprehensible – depending on who you're talking to, or texting. For a face-to-face dialogue, our language has to be clear. In other words, free from other words. Focus on the language that creates a clear picture in your audience's mind. Not only your verbal language, but your body language as well.

Concentrating on gesture patterns or body language is important – how we convey a message relies heavily on body language. But connection with your material through language is the secret to connecting with your audience. It's been my experience that your gestures will get in line, when you are aligned. Body language is a language you already speak. Want to improve your gestures? Then make your presentation matter more to you, and to your listener. Find ways to care more. Review yourself on video, and you can check out the "accent" in your body language!

When I set out to write this book, I didn't want to create a book about giving speeches. I didn't want to discuss voice and diction exercises (there are many alternatives if that is your interest). I didn't want to provide instruction that can be found at Toastmasters or other means. I wanted to create a method of communication that can be applied at a moment's notice, every day. There's no special meeting place, no specific gesture pattern, and no bad Chinese food (what, you've never been to Toastmasters?)

There's only your story, and your connection to your message. That connection is the universal standard for communication. Create a vision and share it with others – there are no magical hand movements; there's only conviction, authenticity and relevance.

The NEW Elevator Pitch is informal, impromptu, and often unexpected. When somebody says, "So, tell me about yourself" or "I'd like to hear more about your ideas", you don't go into Presentation Attack Pattern Zebra-Niner for your response. ("Arms at 10 and 2, begin speaking and fire gesture 26-Alpha for maximum impact! Left hand pincher twist, get ready! You're on deck! ")

PART I: SEVEN STEPS TO CLARITY

Don't start selling. Start connecting.

Remember: You need your listener to say, "Tell Me More..." That's how you earn the right to advance, and you know where you stand. You can correct, instruct, respond or retreat – depending on the feedback you receive.

So, make FEEDBACK your goal! Find out where your audience stands, and where you are, with your ideas. Assert your position in a way that's persuasive, and listen closely for the response. And take your time to lay out your vision in a way that makes your listener say, "Tell me more..."

Taking the time to earn the right to advance, by laying out your main theme with the right language, is the key to your elevator pitch. Ask good questions, at the right time. Expressing yourself, even informally, is a process built on the language of leadership.

YOUR HIGHLIGHT REEL

- Be clear about your themes and your outcomes via the words you use.
- Balance informal speech with a direct approach - avoid clichés
- Use the language of leadership
- Avoid inappropriate judgments
- Use questions to check in with your audience
- Create a dialogue with the NEW Elevator Pitch

Next, you will strengthen your message even further with the most powerful communication tool you have: AUTHENTICITY.

UNDER CONSTRUCTION
CLARITY: Step 2 is Language

Lay out the language that lets your listener know where you are headed. What's your main theme, or idea? Be clear about what you need, and be clear about the language you are using to express that need. Pull out the Pitch Paper that you started in Chapter 1, and add one or two sentences. If you need three, then go for it – we can edit later. Use strong language that lets your audience know what you are about. Lead on!

Step 3

Authenticity

"Trust is our number one asset…as customers learn to trust us, they generate a surprising amount of growth." – *John Brennan, CEO of Vanguard*

"Men will never cast away their dearest pleasures upon the drowsy request of someone who does not even seem to mean what he says." – *Richard Baxter*

"This above all: to thine own self be true,
And it must follow, as the night the day,
Thou canst not then be false to any man."
– Hamlet, *Act I Scene III*

Authenticity: TRUST and Persuasion

On an instinctual level, when we hear a pitch, one of our first thoughts is:

Can I trust this person?

The numbers, the facts, the opinions, the ideas – none of these really matter without trust. Delivering your pitch in person means that you have to connect with the person first of all (that means YOU, and your material) and be completely authentic to your subject and your audience. You have to connect with what really matters, if you want it to matter to anyone else.

The most persuasive communicators inspire trust. They are authentic, and that authenticity leads their audience to action. Trust is the source of persuasion. It's easy to get people to listen to your numbers, facts and opinions – but when they take action, it's because they trust YOU.

Energy

Whether your topic is saving the world, or saving costs on merchandise returns, you must convey trust, first and foremost. Authenticity builds trust. Authenticity is where you walk the walk; your actions match your words, and your elevator speech illustrates your commitment to both your material and your listener. Trust is about more than just being honest; honesty must be a given. Authenticity is about telling the truth, but telling it in a way that makes others say, "Tell me more..."

Authenticity means that you have to connect with you. You have to believe your story, your mission, and your principles with a conviction that is contagious. That's why energy is so important when you deliver your elevator speech. Once you find your "true north" (what you are really all about), you have to SHARE YOUR COMPASS with energy and conviction.

Your pitch must be sincere, if you want others to engage with you.

Authenticity is a commitment.

Your powers of persuasion are linked to your ability to commit to your material.

AUTHENTCITY
Commitment to your material + Commitment to Your Audience = Your Power of Persuasion

---

Real human connection is one of the deepest human needs that we all share; we know it when we see it, and we check out when we don't. The NEW Elevator Pitch is your commitment to your subject, and to your truth. Then, you connect your truth to your audience. The authentic connection is instinctual; we respond to one another at a basic, emotional level when someone is speaking from a place of truth. Surprisingly, many of us are unable to connect effectively with our subject in a way that others view as real, true and authentic.

2:00 Your Two-Minute Drill

Select a statement or phrase about your work that most matters to you and that expresses your most authentic thoughts or beliefs. It can be positive, negative or even ridiculous or silly.

Examples:

- "That last patient was one of the bravest little girls I have ever seen."
- "Nobody cares about which brand of paperclips we use!"
- "There's no one better qualified than Tom for the new European market."
- "No I won't kiss Evelyn for a dollar – and this is not a price negotiation!"

Repeat the phrase three times, changing it if you wish, and feel what it means to be authentic. Do you "buy" you? Are you comfortable practicing with something that you might consider to be a little….goofy? (Maybe it's best to start with something that's not so serious, before you tackle the bigger topics? Ah, poor Evelyn…)

This pitch doesn't have to be an earth-shattering revelation, just as long as it's authentic.

Ready? Set? Start your watch.

Are you energized by your delivery? Do you find yourself connecting with what really matters? Are you able to laugh at yourself? Sometimes being silly is the best way to be authentic. Relax - and your audience will, too!

Overcoming the Inauthentic

Have you ever stopped to wonder why we have all these social media tools like twitter, Google+ and

PART I: SEVEN STEPS TO CLARITY

Facebook? The Social Network (Facebook) is the fastest-growing company since God was a boy, expanding at a rate that can only exist when an organization delivers on a deep-seated human need. That need? The need for us to connect. The NEW Elevator Pitch goes beyond the connections of social media – it has to. A face-to-face conversation is much more authentic than any online connection, if you know how to get it right.

We desperately want to create authentic conversations, conversations where we express ourselves in a way that we recognize as true. While it's true that I had oatmeal for breakfast today (and you can see a picture of the bowl on my profile page), that's not the kind of truth that people crave. Who are you, when times are tough? Who are you, when others are in need? Who are you, when it's time to decide whether to cut the budget or cut headcount? When the conversation matters, it takes courage to define where you stand. The fear that we all feel before we start the NEW Elevator Pitch is a reminder that we need to face up to who we are, and have the courage to share it. Are you committed to making a connection – an authentic connection – with your listener that goes beyond the electronic world of social media?

Presenting Your Authentic Self

How do you communicate your most authentic self? You must touch on the following:

- What you do best and what you enjoy the most –Not good, not better, but BEST is where you want to go for your most authentic elevator pitch. Typically, overcoming obstacles shows us what we can do. Choose what matters most, if you want to make it matter to others!

- What's best for your listeners – challenging the status quo means moving towards a better future – why not choose the one that goes beyond better...all the way to BEST? Your listener is interested in a world where people operate at their best, the best ideas and suggestions are shared, and the best products are compared to the competition. If your pitch covers a product, organization or service, focus on what's best for the customer. Your listener wants to know how you can make a difference; commit to deliver that message! Distinguish yourself by demonstrating a commitment to excellence.

- Conviction – Do you believe that you are the best fit for the position, and that your products are the best fit for the customer? Believe me, you need something to believe in. You know how I know? Because it's human nature. We are all looking for something to believe in. Find the statements that convey your belief, and put that passion into your elevator pitch.

- Reputation – it's one thing to hear what you have to say about you, but what about what others say? Sharing perspectives of those that know you best will help to strengthen your story's authenticity. Similarly, referring to satisfied customers, or to those you have helped, can build a rock-solid and authentic elevator pitch.

Shortlink: http://youtu.be/BSsT-9oyZJk

- Performance – choose the statements that help you to position yourself for the opportunity at hand. For example, if you are interviewing for a team-leader position in finance, it may not be a good idea to say that you are at your best when working on your own on marketing projects. You may want to consider shifting from "I'm at my best when…" to "The solution I'd like to provide is…" to communicate your strengths.

Here are some examples of authentic statements. Think of how you would finish the sentences after the words in bold type. Remember, the words are important, but energy and commitment are what people will hear, first and foremost:

- My greatest accomplishment is building the day-care center from scratch, and helping over 350 kids to be better prepared for kindergarten. Here's how I did it...

- The thing I like (or liked) best about my role at _____ is the opportunity to collaborate with other software developers. I know that I have to take time to code on my own, but sharing ideas has taught me that none of us is as smart as all of us...

- My idea of a great leader is someone who shares the vision, and allows for the input of their trusted advisors. Booker T. Washington said, "Few things can help an individual more than to place responsibility on him and to let him know that you trust him."

- The best way I can help others is through understanding the needs of the team. There's no 'one size fits all' when it comes to leadership, and a one-on-one engagement is key to developing a plan for each employee's personal development....

- One thing I always do to help my [friends/family/co-workers/teammates] is *listen*. It's all too rare for us to really take the time to engage. My teammate, Bob, was having a tough time with the new ERP software and I sat down with him...

2:00 Your Two-Minute Drill

Choose from the list of examples above and include your own responses. Pick one topic, and see if you can deliver a few sentences in two minutes or less. Extra credit if your answer is over 30 seconds long.

- My greatest accomplishment is….
- The thing I like (or liked) best about my role at _____ is/was…..
- My idea of a great leader is someone who….
- The best way I can help others is through….
- One thing I always do to help my [friends/family/co-workers/teammates] is…

You may want to try answering more than one, and keep that information handy when you need authentic personal language to make your point.

Dull and boring pitches are born from disconnected speakers. In contrast, persuading others requires that you communicate in a way that is completely connected – that's authenticity. If you are excited, enthusiastic, angry, or elated, your audience needs to SEE and HEAR the connection. Your emotions are translated through authenticity: a real connection with your subject, and your audience.

YOUR HIGHLIGHT REEL

Don't waste your listener's time with dull emotions, phoniness, or other elevator-stalling techniques.

- Authenticity delivers truth and develops trust
- Everyone craves a real connection – authenticity provides one
- Authenticity must be consistent: match your meaning to your message
- Connect with your subject, if you want your audience to do the same

Remember the old saying, "people don't care about how much you know; they want to know how much you care". Put caring into every part of your pitch, by talking about what matters. Be authentic, to be heard.

UNDER CONSTRUCTION

CLARITY: Step 3 is Authenticity

Authenticity is hard to convey in a sentence or two, because it's a style element that has to be a part of your entire pitch.

Pull out your "Pitch Paper" and add Authenticity to the mix.

What sentences can you come up with that show you are really connected to your material? How will you gain trust by delivering truth? Show that you care, and connect, with the words that help you most.

Relevance

"Be who you are and say what you feel because those who mind don't matter and those who matter don't mind." – *Dr. Seuss*

"People don't buy WHAT you do, they buy WHY you do it" – *Simon Sinek*

"As you grow, you don't change into someone else…you become more of who you already are." – *Marcus Buckingham*

The NEW Elevator Pitch is obviously something important to you; you care about what you say. So, here's the next question: Why should someone else care? Making your story relevant is the key to driving meaningful change. Persuasion relies on relevance; your ideas must be compelling (right here, right now) or your listener says, "So what?"

The key to relevance is making what matters to you, matter to others.

Why You Need Relevance

In my work with colleges and universities, I run into a lot of super tech-savvy folks. The Millennial Generation has grown up with the Internet, and as a result they can instantly access a world of information. What they have a harder time doing is sifting through that information to make it relevant. While it's true that any resourceful person has access to the same set of facts on the web, there's still more to the story. What about interpreting those facts? How about summarizing the information into salient (meaningful) data – in a way that helps the organization to make its next move (or next 12 moves...). Access alone is not enough; being able to get to the information doesn't always mean you can provide relevant answers.

Getting to Why

Even with the magic of Google at your disposal, finding the information that matters -right now- can be a challenge. Especially if that information relies on your experience. A well-crafted elevator speech can accelerate the process in powerful ways.

You see, I just Googled "your experience" and, while I got a lot of hits, none of them really address what I need: Namely, the experience that is uniquely yours. Your experience is not indexed in a search engine. The combined powers of Google, Twitter and YouTube still can't interpret the data in the same way as you can – and you can do it in less than two minutes! The NEW Elevator

Pitch goes beyond the information on the web – if you know how to make it relevant.

Relevant information explains to your audience why you, and why this, and why now. Relevance can address any of the following:

- Why you want the job
- Why your screenplay is going to be a hit
- Why your company offers these services
- Why the listener should care (e.g.: The inventory is out of control. Why does that matter to me?)

Even if your elevator pitch is to a team of investors, or a sales team where "all that matters are the numbers", you ALWAYS have to answer why:

- **Why You?**
- Why are these the numbers – why should we believe your projections?
- Why this strategy?
- Why are your choices are the best, and why should we follow you?

The day-to-day issues of your pitch don't become relevant until you get to "why". If your pitch is a personal story, the "why" is the heart of the matter, literally and figuratively. People want to know why before they buy.

> We all try to maximize our value based on what we can offer, what we enjoy, and what really matters to us. What really matters is why.

2:00 Your Two-Minute Drill
What's Your Why?

Take a moment to consider why you are delivering your elevator pitch. You know your desired outcomes (sell more stuff, get the job, help the team, solve a business issue, etc.). You know your strengths ("I'm at my best when…" "Others will tell you that I'm ….") but why are these things important to your listener? How can you phrase your why in terms of others?

Consider adding one or more of the phrases below for your pitch. Which one(s) do you like best? Or, do you have one of your own?

- "Let me tell you why I'm passionate about…"
- "The thing that matters most to me [or, "all of us", or "the organization"] is _____, and here's why…."
- "Maybe people will say that I care too much, but I've been dedicated to _____ for a very long time. That's why…."
- "Working with Habitat for Humanity has meant the world to me, and here's why…"

Ready? Start your timer.

PART I: SEVEN STEPS TO CLARITY

Because…and Why It Works

Think back to when you were a kid and you'd ask your mother or father, "Why is the sky blue? Why do people call it a 'no-brainer'? Why should I clean up my room? Why _____?" The classic response? BECAUSE.

"Because…" is a classic strategy that's worked for parents since kids could talk. I agree with author Simon Sinek: let's start with why…but don't forget to move quickly to "because".

Here's a classic strategy to deliver a persuasive "why" – all based on the power of BECAUSE: In a Harvard study, researcher Ellen Langer wanted to understand how to create influence and compliance. Her team of researchers went out to libraries, and asked to cut in line to use the copy machine with a simple question:

"Excuse me, May I use the Xerox machine?
I have to make 5 copies"

What do you think: what percentage of patrons allowed the researchers to cut in line?

Typically, when I ask this "What percentage said 'yes'?" question, I get the following responses from the group:

Canada:	80% or more
Atlanta:	70%
Texas:	50%
Chicago:	33%
Florida:	20%
India:	10%
New Jersey:	*Fuhgettaboutit*

The actual number? 60%.

In Langer's study, six times out of 10, the researchers were allowed to cut in and make five copies. So, Langer decided to change the question – and see if the results changed. The new question was:

"Excuse me, May I use the Xerox machine?
I have to make 5 copies, because I'm in a hurry"

What do you think happened to the percentages? Up, down, or remain at 60%?

The responses went up – WAY up! The results changed -- to 94%! Are you surprised?

Was "Because" the key to agreement? Langer wanted to be sure; like all good researchers, the team wanted to eliminate the variables in their experiment.

The team suggested that it was the "in a hurry" part that was skewing the results. So, they changed the experiment. Now the question was:

**"Excuse me, May I cut in line?
I have to make 5 copies, because... I have to make copies"**

Obvious, and kinda dumb, right? What do you think happened?

The results changed – but only by 1%! That's right – the researchers were still allowed to cut in line 93% of the time! Clearly, "Because" created compliance – that one word was the catalyst in this experiment.

Taking it one step further, Langer's team decided to increase the number of copies from 5 to 20, to see if "Because" really was a magic word. The result? The percentages dropped dramatically, below 30%. Asking to make 20 copies was too much – it wasn't realistic. Even with a good reason, the inconvenience was too much to overcome. The expectations were unacceptable.

If your elevator pitch asks the equivalent of "making 20 copies", learn from Langer. Break down your objective into component parts, if you want to win. The NEW Elevator Pitch is, at best, a couple of minutes in length. Why try to fit in 20 pages? Break down your story, so that it's easy for your audience to say "yes" to it. Work on getting a 94% success rate by showing how your solution is realistic, achievable, and easily acceptable.

Realistic Expectations

Perhaps a gentleman will be inspired to try this approach, with a member of the opposite sex: "Excuse me. I'd like you to come home with me BECAUSE..."

Thinking of trying this technique?

All I can say is: remember, REALISTIC EXPECTATIONS.

"Because" is not a magic word, but it's an important one.

People have to believe that your request is realistic or the best "Because..." in the world won't help you. In order to believe in your request, people have to believe in you. They have to see your authentic connection to "why" and "because". How can you make it easy to say "yes" to your persuasive idea, even when that idea may be inconvenient for the listener?

And: Why would you go for 20 pages – when your success rate is above 93%, if you try for 5? Why not go for five, four times? Think about it – and be brief if you want to hear a "YES!"

PART I: SEVEN STEPS TO CLARITY

Too Much Information

One of the most common mistakes in an elevator speech comes from over-engineering the pitch. Too much information doesn't leave room for someone to say, "Tell me more…" In fact, it makes your listener say, "Tell me LESS!" a version of TMI (too much information) that doesn't serve you at all.

What is your "because" in terms of how your solution changes things for the better, for your listener? How much data or detail do you really need to support that theme, in your pitch?

When they say, "Tell me more…" what will you tell them?

What question(s) do you want to be asked at the end of your pitch?

What would you do or say to prompt those questions?

Relevance is about choosing the words that help you most: edit your thoughts and ideas into bullet points, to create your why and demonstrate your because. Leave room for questions, and consider possible outcomes if you want your story to be clear.

One way to avoid over-talking, and keep the conversation relevant is to focus on what you want your listener to do when you finish.

Find Out Their Why

If you reach the end of your pitch, and you don't get the anticipated response, FIND OUT WHY. If your listener asks you a question that is off-topic, best to respond, but then – re-focus the attention on the issues that you feel are most important.

There's always an alternative to any persuasive pitch, no matter how compelling. In addition to "do something else" (hire a different person, buy a different product, invest in a different company), there's always "do nothing". Why is "do nothing" the wrong answer? What is your call to action? Why now? Find the urgency. Create relevance by probing:

- "I thought for sure you would be curious about the first-year projections. Does that mean you agree completely with my assumptions?"

- "You haven't asked about the dollar figure required for the first round of funding. May I ask why?"

- "Your question about our European warehouse is interesting. For me, we've got such rampant issues here on the East Coast that I believe we need to focus our attention domestically. Based on the size of the inventory and the customer base, I believe that our US operations are much more relevant to our profitability....and here's why..."

- "I thought you might have been curious to know more about my e-tailing experience. I believe my web design background could bring some real value to the online division at Pier1, because I've handled strategic design for JCPenney's website. How does my background at JCPenney fit for your vision of the position?"

Confirmation from your listener means that you have earned the right to advance, so be ready for the follow-up that advances your objectives. Pushback is a possibility. (For example, if you are going to mention JCPenney's web initiatives as a selling point, get ready to be asked some hard questions about the sanctions that Google imposed on Penney's in 2011...Penney's aggressive tactics in search engine optimization were not a source of pride for the company).

Prepare for the continuance you seek. Still, leaving room for questions can make the control freak, freak.

"Q&A? YIKES!! What will they ask? How will I respond? What if they go somewhere that I haven't researched?" Fair questions, one and all. Consider: You have to stay especially relevant during the dialogue that follows your elevator speech. Think about the questions you anticipate – the ones that you want, and the ones that you dread. Ask a friend or a coach to ask you the tough questions, and include a curveball or two just to help you deal with potential surprises.

2:00 Your Two-Minute Drill

Remember, the NEW Elevator Pitch is a two-minute drill: there is information that you are going to leave out! Find someone you don't know very well and practice your pitch. Maybe a person on an airplane, a cabdriver, or the parents of one of your kid's friends. How does it feel to give your pitch to someone, when the stakes aren't all that high?

When you practice your pitch, does your "rehearsal partner" give you the response you want? Why, or why not? Go ahead, you better ask. What have you got to lose?

Ready? Set? Start your timer.

Are there cues you should have given to your listener, to get the response you want? What language cues can you give to your listener? Choose the words (and the cues!) that help you most, and get ready to dive deeper on those topics. Check out the "Informal Pitch" scenario at the end of the book, to see some more ideas.

Be Prepared

Preparation helps us avoid delivering too much information. Preparation is the antidote to nerves. Fear is an internal memo from your brain, letting you know that you need to be prepared.

Being prepared is just good sense – it will help you to be more confident in your pitch, and in the conversation that follows.

Creating relevance relies on your ability to convey four simple words with clarity and conviction, when you want to persuade. Here they are:

I've thought this through.

Whether your elevator pitch is a personal introduction, or product overview, you have to consider your audience. How does your solution improve the status quo, and encourage your listener to take action? If your ideas are relevant and necessary, what obstacles could prevent you from getting a "YES"?

Shortlink: http://youtu.be/obtdeZZwzoA

Dialogue

The NEW Elevator Pitch is a dialogue; as we've addressed before – and if you are being asked to defend your position or explain your beliefs, you are right on track! Even if your listener confronts you with a, "Tell me more…about your crazy ideas!"

Expect curiosity, and be prepared for possible outcomes.

Curiosity takes many forms – it can be challenging, and even aggressive, depending on the situation and personalities in the room. So…. "how am I supposed to respond to these questions?" you may wonder. Remember the process so far, and apply it to your responses:

CAPTIVATE your audience with a quick introduction.

LANGUAGE helps guide your listener towards your desired conclusion.

AUTHENTICITY is your true connection to your subject.

RELEVANCE is about making what matters to you, matter to your listener.

The NEW Elevator Pitch is a process for communication – not always a rehearsed speech. The strategies that apply to your pitch also apply to your responses – because the formula of the seven steps is about effective communication. You will accelerate your conversations, because now you know how to make what matters to you, matter to your listener.

YOUR HIGHLIGHT REEL

To be relevant,

- Start with why
- Move to because
- Make your request realistic and achievable
- Avoid too much information, by concentrating on what matters to your listener, and focusing on getting them to ask, "Tell Me More…"

How have you "thought this through" - are you ready for the challenges that are relevant to you?

In the upcoming chapters, we'll look more closely at how to shift your attention to your listener – how to INSPIRE the response you want, address it with TACT, and move towards "YES!"

UNDER CONSTRUCTION

CLARITY: Step 4 is Relevance

This section could be as simple as your "why" and your "because" – two powerful sentences that can create the relevance you need.

STEP 3: AUTHENTICITY

Pull out your "Pitch Paper" and ask yourself, "How can I make sure my message is relevant?" Write down your answer and add it to your pitch. Can you convey your message in a way that makes it important to your audience?

Inspiration

"No knot unties itself" – *from* "Into the Woods"

"If you want to understand inspiration, it's going to take some doing." *- from* Inspiration: Your Ultimate Calling *by Dr. Wayne Dyer*

Defining the Term, "Inspiration"

Inspiration, in the NEW Elevator Pitch, means the process of being mentally stimulated to do or feel something, especially something creative. Inspiration leads to action; inspiring your listener takes your elevator pitch out of the commonplace and into the rare. While "what you say" is very important, what your listener does is most important of all. What Dr. Dyer says is true – inspiration requires some doing. Your ability to inspire is not based on what you say during your pitch, but what the listener does after your pitch is done.

Ask 100 people what inspires them, and you will get 100 different answers.

In fact, based on my research, the specific breakdown goes like this:

What inspires you? 100 People Surveyed	Responses
Things in nature ("the mountains" "going to the beach"):	19
Answers that belong on a poster with an eagle ("Achievement" "Going the distance"):	16
Family answers ("my kids" "my husband" "my baby's smile"):	12
Experiential responses ("Being in church" "Listening to music"):	11
Other ("I have no idea" "Please leave me alone" "Who are you again?"):	44
TOTAL:	100

What inspires you? More importantly: What inspires your listener?

Positive Change

Whether you are inspired by natural beauty, a child's smile, great music or a religious experience, all inspirational events have one thing in common.

Inspiration comes from positive change.

You hear a great song, and your mood changes. We are moved to action by that positive impulse that comes from a favorite tune. The music can inspire you to get back to making dinner, or back to working on your blog post. Watch your mood shift during a walk along a beautiful beach.   A business man who had an awful day, losing millions in the stock market, is instantly inspired when his son says, "Can we play now, Daddy?"   Often the most brilliant ideas are the simplest.   Inspiration, even in the face of difficulty, can come from even the slightest change in our perspective.

If you seek to inspire your listener, seek to create that positive change by challenging the status quo. Quickly and effectively, you must show how current circumstances will change for the better, based on your ideas.

Transformation is the source of your inspiration.

Know the change you want to make.
Know the action you want your listener to take.

Inspiration and Motivation

Inspiration is a lot like motivation – we all have it, but it's impossible to truly share it. I mean, what is "your motivation"?   Could you put it in an envelope and send it to me please? Could we bake it into a meatloaf, or put it in the back seat of your car?

Like all emotional states, motivation and inspiration are words that can only be understood through action. If a crying woman just keyed someone's car, we might comment that she is motivated by jealousy and/or anger – but can we be sure it's not something else? When someone is laughing at the end of the movie, or getting up at 4:30 am to go fishing, we might have a pretty good idea of what inspires them – but still, the reasons can't be known with exact certainty. Inspiration is murky, but actions are crystal clear.

Action

Actions trump salesmanship in every elevator pitch. While style matters, it's the action that you inspire that will ultimately measure your effectiveness. After you've captured your audience's attention, you talk about what you've done, and what you're doing, in the context of "why" and "because", so that you establish relevance. Moving towards the end of the pitch, you've gotten past "So what?" and the next question is, "Now what?" Your audience wants to know:

"What are you going to do next?"

Or, even better, "What are we going to do together?"

Shortlink: http://goo.gl/mr7qC

PART I: SEVEN STEPS TO CLARITY

You understand the importance of why, and because, to demonstrate your authentic gifts in a way that is relevant to the listener. Now that you've made your case, what do you want the listener to do?

Leadership and Inspiration

Earlier, I wrote about your LANGUAGE – laying out the path you want your listener to follow. You understand why, and because. But how can someone phrase an outcome in a way that is both positive and realistic? Remember, unrealistic is undesirable in the NEW Elevator Pitch. What honest results can your listener expect, by following your lead? As you move to INSPIRATION, consider the anticipated results for your audience. For example:

- Approving this new budget means that over 500 children in the village will receive food and shelter for the winter months.

- Adjusting your mortgage means you can save $26,000 over the life of the loan. Your closing costs will pay for themselves in savings in just 22 months.

- Signing the lease on the warehouse will allow us to realize the projections for Europe next year. The market remains uncertain, but without this investment the only certainty is that our European business won't be able to grow.

By choosing the right language, leaders inspire positive action.

Creativity

In a recent survey called, "Capitalizing on Complexity", IBM surveyed 1,541 global CEOs. They asked this elite group what qualities they look for in employees, in order to better cope with the new economy. According to these CEOs, the most important leadership quality isn't technical competence, loyalty, or financial skills. The most important leadership quality is creativity.

Creativity in the IBM context doesn't mean "arts and crafts"; it doesn't mean that the best leaders are in marketing or advertising (although they could be), or that sculptors should quit their day job and enter the corporate arena. The survey explains that we have to understand creativity as the process of creation: the ability to make something new, to create something that hasn't happened before.

Inspiration is the centerpiece of creativity (the process of creation).

Your elevator pitch is designed to persuade – but, to persuade what, exactly? What is it that you would like to create - *with, through or for your listener*?

2:00 Your Two-Minute Drill

Use this exercise to spur your creativity.

What inspires you? Why? And, do you really think that butterflies and whiskers on kittens will help your elevator pitch? (Keep it relevant to the issues at hand!)

Make a list of triggers that could inspire your listener. You may be surprised to find that you come up with a potential "hook" that will captivate the listener, at the beginning of your speech (BONUS!)

Possible Triggers – Examples:
- Helping grow the business
- Serving the common good (social causes)
- Investing in quality people and products
- Reaching more students and expanding learning opportunities
- Electing a candidate with a real recipe for fiscal responsibility

What will inspire your audience to take action, and overcome the natural impulse to do nothing? See how many triggers you can come up with in 2 minutes.

Inspiration is a shapeless concept; after all, it's different for everybody. You can't know what inspires me. But you can know what you want to create. The world you want to create is the source of your inspiration; share that with your audience, in no uncertain terms.

Inspiration creates action. Focusing on results will take your conversation from information to inspiration, and help your listener to understand what is needed. Create a clear and compelling call to action for your audience as shown in these examples.

Examples of Inspirational Closes:

"Getting the two candidates together with a room full of young decision makers will benefit the city, and the Recreation Center. We have the resources and the venue; our next steps are securing the funding from our top five donors. Do you see any obstacles to moving forward with this plan?"

"Creating digital campaigns at Best Buy allowed my team to grow the business by almost $576 million over six years. Based on what we've discussed, there's a similar opportunity here at Lowe's. The documents in front of you will outline the initial costs in building the team. As you look it over, I'd like you to consider the investment in terms of the potential revenues over the next several quarters. We can make this change happen..."

"The new Salamander Technology means that your cell phone now becomes your credit card. No more wallets, no more cash. The third screen just became a transaction tool. But today, we still need to get your wallets involved, if we want to make this dream a reality. With your investment of $1.6 million, we can finalize the software and bring this product to market in less than 120 days."

"Ever since she was third-runner-up on American Idol last year, we've continued to watch her audience grow, not shrink. We've built an authentic following and they are hungry for more downloads. You've heard the demo tracks - both country and pop – and you know that is exactly what the market wants, right now. We can deliver the goods; we just need your green light to get into the San Francisco studios next month."

Being clear about what you need is the key to creating positive change through others. Speaking with clarity means helping others to find inspiration through clear guidance, direction and expectations. You pitch has a purpose: inspiration is the way to communicate your intentions. It's a vital step in the process of getting to "YES!"

YOUR HIGHLIGHT REEL

- Inspiration comes from positive change.
- The number one quality in business is creativity – the power to create new solutions in the face of adversity.
- Actions speak louder than words – especially words like "motivation". Be crystal-clear on the action you

want the listener to take – to move towards an inspiring future that you create together.

- Make your close inspirational

Positive change and positive action are compelling, but in order to deliver on the promise of your pitch, you have to include one more over-arching element before you reach your goal. You have to understand how to make your inspirational message appropriate for your audience. You have to communicate with TACT.

UNDER CONSTRUCTION

CLARITY: Step 5 is Inspiration

By now, your Pitch Paper is taking shape. You've got the main ideas and themes – now it's time to move towards your audience, and focus on what matters to them. Craft one or two sentences, designed to inspire the action that you want, and write them down. Your Pitch Paper is almost complete. How do you like it so far?

Next up: overcoming challenges with the NEW Elevator Pitch requires TACT: How to make your message appropriate, even if it's difficult to hear.

Tact

"Tact is the art of making a point without making an enemy." – *Isaac Newton*

"Each of us must learn when the time fits the response and must tailor our action or reaction to each situation... Constantly criticizing yourself for past mistakes and errors tends to precipitate the very thing you would like to avoid."
– *Vince Lombardi*

"The key is to communicate your feelings in a way that invites and encourages the recipient to consider new ways of behaving, rather than suggesting they're a schmuck and it's too bad there's nothing they can do about it."
– *from* Difficult Conversations, *Stone/Patton/Heen*

No presentation is complete without tact and diplomacy. Saying the right thing at the right time in the right way is the essence of tact, and the key to landing your message. Especially if the message is difficult to hear.

Shortlink: http://bit.ly/vseApU

Tact: Knowing What to Say, When to Say It, and How to Say It.

In the NEW Elevator Pitch, it's important to understand your material. It's important to know why, and to communicate "because" in a way that is compelling to your listener. These aspects are all part of your pre-work, your practice time and two-minute drills. But during your pitch, it's critical that you understand one element, and one element only, if you've done your homework so far. You have to understand your audience. Consider what your audience will respond to at the beginning ...and at the end. When to say your key theme is equally important.

When the timing is inappropriate, the remarks go beyond "charming", past "disarming" and become "alarming". Your pitch may seem inappropriate. You cut off the listener from drawing their own conclusions when you force-feed them yours. This approach is also called the "hard sell".

PART I: SEVEN STEPS TO CLARITY

They say there's no such thing as a bad question, but there is such a thing as bad timing.

Consider this one question which, if asked at the appropriate time, can yield phenomenal results. But, if you haven't earned the right to advance, you are WAAAAY out of line. Ready? Here goes:

"Will you marry me?"

There's a lot of work that goes into that one simple remark, those four words that can quite literally change your life (or break your heart!) depending on the response. And timing is crucial.

Tact Takes a Holiday

In order to be tactful, you have to be confident. You cannot deliver a message that is in tune with your audience if you are having an attack of nerves.

While the NEW Elevator Pitch is an informal presentation, usually delivered to individuals or small groups, nerves can still come into play – even for a presentation pro. You don't have to be speaking to a large audience to feel jittery; if you are meeting with your boss, or an angel investor, or a film producer, one important person is enough to raise the stakes. If your subject is something that really matters to you (e.g.: getting a raise, acquiring a multi-million dollar investment) then you can bet that the adrenaline will be flowing. While it's not possible to eliminate fear entirely, focusing on your audience is the key to getting beyond your nervousness. Sometimes nerves can manifest in strange ways: leaving out an important point, or getting frustrated when your point isn't being heard. Sometimes we pull back when we want to push ahead. When our actions are out of sync with the demands of the moment, we aren't delivering the right message at the right time. We are losing our tact, and our listener may be losing patience.

In my coaching practice, some of my clients often view presentations with a deep-seated fear. Anxiety is a part of modern life, wouldn't you agree? But - before we reach into the medicine cabinet for answers - let's look at how can we take action, in spite of our nerves, and create a message that is meaningful, compelling, and tactful.

Overcoming Nerves: Find Out More Online at http://pitchthefear.com

Public speaking is not a matter of life and death, although some may think so. In order to understand how to overcome the natural fear associated with a high-stakes presentation, I reached out to some folks who have to conquer fear on a daily basis, in order to do their jobs. I believe that we can learn a lot from people who deal with high-pressure situations, and apply their strategies to our own lives. Perspective is an important part of dealing with fear; here's one for you to consider:

PART I: SEVEN STEPS TO CLARITY

Kevin Molitor is a firefighter and EMT (Emergency Medical Technician) in the suburbs of Chicago. He's not famous; he's not a politician, preacher or rock star. He's a guy whose business is saving lives, every day. Kevin typically rides with a special ambulance crew that can be dispatched to traditional medical emergencies, or to fire and accident scenes. On a regular basis, his job requires him to:

- Put himself in danger to rescue people who have been injured in car crashes or fires – including underwater rescues (he's certified for SCUBA)
- Make decisions about how to treat traumas before putting a patient into the ambulance – decisions that, if incorrect, could cause harm, injury or even death
- Enter into burning buildings, frozen rivers and other extremely dangerous places in order to save lives

While Kevin has undergone extensive training for a variety of emergency situations, there is always an 'x-factor' of unknown potential harm. Kevin often finds himself in clear and present danger, and yet he has to move forward. "You see the slogans on t-shirts," Kevin says, "you know, 'We Fight What You Fear'. But, without any fear, you'd get yourself into situations you couldn't get yourself out of. There's always fear, anybody who says they aren't afraid isn't telling you the whole story. But you focus on your training, you focus on the job at hand, if you want to save a life (including your own)."

According to Kevin, focusing on your fear only makes it stronger. Overcoming fear is a matter of focus, and reliance on expert training. Here was his secret to turning fear into action:

Make the other person's situation more important than your own.

Like all firefighters, Kevin took an oath to serve – an oath that he takes very seriously. His commitment outweighs any other emotions he may be feeling, and it keeps him focused on being safe. Ultimately, he believes that what he has to do is more important than what he feels inside. While some may consider Kevin a hero, he says he's just a guy with a job to do. He has been decorated by the fire department more than once for his courage under fire (Yes that is my Very. Best. Pun. Ever.)

As a young sales executive at AT&T, I was listening to a presentation by my sales manager. He was explaining all the various products and services that were available to our customers, and going into details on a wide array of solutions. My brain began to go into overload, and I started to worry. What if I didn't remember the various data points in front of the customer? How could I be persuasive, if I didn't bring out every key point, every feature, and every benefit? I raised my hand.

"What am I supposed to do if I can't remember all this stuff, in front of the customer? Which product should be first, or third? I guess I'm just wondering: Where should I focus?"

The sales manager's reply was a piece of advice I've never forgotten. "Always focus on the customer." You can overcome your fear of presentations by focusing on your audience.

Courage

While we all know how to speak, and we all know how to have a conversation, we need to take time to drill and practice if we want to be truly compelling. Persuasive pitches are natural for the very few; most of us have to practice to put our fear aside. If nerves are your body's way of saying, "You need to rehearse!" then you better listen. Your audience could be your boss, your CEO, your Board of Directors, or your future wife! The stakes are high, in the NEW Elevator Pitch, when the result matters to you. How can you make the results matter to others?

Following Kevin's advice, it's time to make the listener more important than your fear. To get you used to practicing, I've included three Two-Minute Drills in this chapter. Time to get to work!

2:00 Your Two-Minute Drills

Drill #1:

Take out a sheet of paper; draw a line down the center so you have two columns. On the left-hand side of the page, write out all of the things that make you nervous about delivering your pitch.

Write out everything that comes to mind, no matter how absurd. What's your worst-case scenario? What's the littlest (and biggest) thing you're nervous about?

On the right-hand column, write out your "why" and "because" statements, in terms of your audience.

Ok, take a break. That should have taken two minutes. It's important to go quickly, and not overthink things. It's an elevator speech, not surgery, and what comes to mind first is often best in these drills. Keep your piece of paper, and let's keep going with Drill #2. Ready?

PART I: SEVEN STEPS TO CLARITY

Drill #2: Fear Fighter: Alignment

Makes Me Nervous	What Really Matters
My voice sounds weird (2) They won't like the idea (1) Terry is going to laugh (3) Someone may throw a tomato (4)	Funding the project Helping the kids Engaging the community Putting some fun into the new project Improving the school district

Back to the left side: Assign a "reality" scale to your fears. Put a "1" next to every item that is realistic and likely, "4" for the unlikely or ridiculous.

Based on the real fears on the left hand side (1), what can you do to minimize these concerns? What steps can you take to reduce these fears?

- Turn on the video camera and rehearse?
- Hire a coach?
- Ask a trusted friend for feedback on your pitch?

No action means no change. Practice and action are the antidote for fear. Remember, action defines courage, according to Kevin. What action will you take to make sure your elevator pitch isn't stuck on the first floor, just because of your nerves?

Drill #3: Fear Fighter: Strengthen Your Story

Based on the "why" and "because" statements: is your right hand column stronger (and more important to

110

you) than the left? What could you do to care more about your objectives than your fears?

Possible answers include:

- Re-write your why and because statements, to make them stronger
- Consider what happens if you don't persuade your listener. Isn't being persuasive more important than being afraid?
- Focus on success: What happens when you win? What are the next logical steps, if you succeed?

The Empty Chair

Hard conversations can sometimes cancel out tactfulness, when the gloves come off and personalities come forward. You know what I mean?

Comments can lead to questions that lead to allegations that lead to agendas that never seem to align. When the conversation matters, people get invested, and they get involved – with energy that can be unsettling, if unexpected. In order to keep your cool, and keep focused on your agenda, you have to have a way to remain tactful even when others aren't. In the face of charged remarks and a heated elevator pitch, I like to remember the concept of the Empty Chair. The Empty Chair represents the person (or persons) who can't be in the room for your conversation, even though the results could have a profound impact on their lives, their professions or their families. The Empty Chair is the seat at the table for the customer, the shareholder, the patient, the front-line manager or the student – the folks whose lives will be deeply touched by the results of the NEW Elevator Pitch. Consider the change you want to make, and who that change is really designed to help. Often, heated dialogue leaves out the person or persons who are the focus for the business (or the charity, the university, or the hospital. You get the idea). The Empty Chair is reserved for the person who gets left out, when agendas and frustrations overtake a difficult conversation.

You see, the NEW Elevator Pitch is designed for difficult conversations. Turbulence is expected. Every elevator pitch is about creating change, and disrupting the status quo in some way. People resist change. People don't like change, even when it's good for them.

What's good is not always what's familiar, and that unfamiliarity breeds resistance.

Consider the Empty Chair, in the face of change. What does your proposed change mean for your listener – and for the person who's not in the room? Resistance can cause us to lose focus. Remember what matters, no matter what. Ask your listener to consider the person that will be impacted by your proposed change. Help your listener to see an important audience, even when they can't be in the room with you. Put someone in the Empty Chair, as a reminder to keep the conversation on track, even when emotions come into play.

Check In and Get Your Bearings

Feeling lost? Feeling nervous? Do you feel you have lost touch with your audience? The clues you need are right in front of you. Your customer is your audience, your listener. If you get lost, focus on your listener. If you aren't sure if your solution is a fit, focus on your listener. The NEW Elevator Pitch is a dialogue, not a sermon. Our social media messages are best when they are interactive; why wouldn't the NEW Elevator Pitch be the exact same way?

Questions Force Interactivity

There are two types of "check-in" questions. Close-ended Questions ask the listener for a "yes" or "no" answer. Open-ended questions offer the listener an opportunity to describe their response in more detail, without the use of a short yes-or-no answer.

Close-Ended vs. Open-Ended: Which Is Better?

Close-ended questions are used to confirm (or deny) your progress so far. Because the responses are quick, they can be a perfect fit for the NEW Elevator Pitch. Confirmation indicates forward movement, and helps you to earn the right to advance. But trust your instincts: does "yes" really mean "yes"? If you have concerns, don't be afraid to dig deeper. What you have to say is important; what your listener is going to <u>do</u> is crucial. Here is a list of some check in questions.

> - "Does what I've said so far make sense for your organization?"
> - "Is this investment in line with your portfolio goals?"
> - "Based on what you've heard: do you believe that Alex can improve the school system here in Baltimore?"

Powerful Questions

Often, a close-ended question can be combined with an open-ended one, to help your listener to elaborate on their last comment. Open-ended questions begin with some version of "How..." "What..." or "Why..." - an inquiry that encourages the listener to expand on an idea and elaborate on their reasoning. While some are hesitant to use these questions ("What if my elevator pitch runs over two minutes?") I say it's better to put down the stopwatch and pick up the business. But that doesn't mean that you can ramble. Be concise if you want to be heard. Practice a two-minute drill. Play until you win.

When people ask, "How long should I let others speak, when they respond to my questions?" The right answer is: As long as it takes for you to win. Better to watch your customer than to watch the clock. Your audience's response is your objective. Get your listener engaged, to get to your objective. Further guidance from your listener can help you to earn the right to advance, or address a challenge head-on, in your pitch.

114

- "How does that last remark fit for your vision of the position?"
- "What would change here at ESPN, if you were to add this show to the fall lineup?"
- "Why would MD Anderson invest in this brand of research, versus a more traditional method?"

The Power of "NO"

Sometimes, even our best pitches don't get the response we want. "NO" is a great teacher. As Michael Neill says in his book *Supercoach*, making it OK to say "NO" gives us the opportunity to be open to new learning and new information. That is, if we can keep from getting furious about not getting our way.

A negative response is an enormous CLUE from your listener. While you may view a negative as discouraging news, consider it an informational bulletin. "No" is a message that class is in session. Pay attention! When you hear a "no", it's your turn to say, "Tell Me More…" Find out why your pitch is not a fit. You could find that you can adjust your solution to the lesson at hand, if you listen to any objections and can correct your approach. "No" really means:

- You are about to learn more about something crucial to your pitch: listen closely!
- There's something you've left out. What is it?
- There's a hidden concern or agenda that you have failed to address. What is it?

PART I: SEVEN STEPS TO CLARITY

- Your solution may not be a fit. So: What is?
- If the listener's expectations are unrealistic, even a genie or Kris Kringle can't help you. You have to have a clear definition of success, based on the solution you can provide.

Learn what you can. Address what you can fix. Understand that not every pitch is a fit for every situation. Finding the right situation is sometimes a process of education. Ultimately, if your pitch is not a fit for your listener, you need to walk away with a greater understanding of why your solution is not a fit – so that you can be better prepared for the next conversation.

"But," I can hear you thinking, "if they say no, my [invention won't get made/ I won't get the sale/the screenplay gets put on the shelf/we can't produce the CD]! How can I be OK with NO, when what I want is 'YES'?"

No Way

First of all, being "OK" with "NO" doesn't mean that you work towards it. It doesn't mean that you celebrate "NO" with a small office party, a parade, or even an extra cup of coffee. Do not expect a negative response, but PREPARE for it. Being prepared means that you learn from "NO" so it doesn't derail your elevator. Like a signpost that says, "Turn right here."

"NO" can mean "not now." "NO" can mean, "not here". "NO" can mean, "not for us." Think of "NO" as a detour to yes. It's up to you to find out what where "NO" leads you; it's up to you to assign meaning to a negative response.

Ask yourself: Have you done everything you can to get to "YES"? Do you know the why and because, behind the "NO"? While you may not like the negative response, can you accept it, learn from it, and find another place and time that's right for you, your story, and your ideas? After all, if I quit after the first "NO," I never would have done much of anything with my life. (Or my wife, come to think of it.)

Focusing on the audience is crucial to your message. In fact, focusing on the audience is so important, because it's the secret to overcoming any nerves in your presentation.

YOUR HIGHLIGHT REEL

Tact means saying the right thing, at the right time, in the right way. Don't let anger or fears stop your elevator; expect that change will be difficult in some way

Fear is a question of focus. Eliminate fear by staying focused:
- Focus on the customer (your listener)
- Focus on the task at hand (delivering your pitch)
- Focus on your outcomes (getting to "YES!" – and, look at the next chapter – that's exactly where we are)

While you've considered the prospect of no agreement and you've prepared by considering the empty chair and other tactics from this chapter, our next step is about moving towards success. What happens when you reach agreement, and how do you know when you've hit your objective for the NEW Elevator Pitch? The action that you want is a "YES!" from your audience, and that's exactly what's coming up next.

UNDER CONSTRUCTION

CLARITY: Step 6 is Tact

What's the right message for your audience? Your Pitch Paper needs some tact, especially if you pitch is a difficult message. There are some great examples and ideas in the Scenarios section, if you are having trouble with TACT. But for now, try out one or two sentences that can help convey courage, as well as a clear direction for your listener. Update your Pitch Paper - one more chapter to go!

YES!

Finding Agreement

"Think about how you would feel walking into a job interview with no other job offers – only some uncertain leads. Think about how the talk about salary would go. Now contrast that with how you would feel walking in with two other job offers. How would that salary negotiation proceed?"
– *Roger Fisher and William Ury*, Getting to YES

"Be careful what you wish for – you just might get it." – *Proverb*

Preparation is the key to making a persuasive argument. Preparation helps you to connect to what matters, and preparation will convey your concerns to your listener. Yet, there's one aspect of preparation we've yet to address. You also have to prepare for success.

What happens when you finish your pitch, your listener – your VIP audience with the power to make your change happen - goes beyond, "Tell Me More...?" and says... "YES!"

- YES, let's fund the project!
- YES, you would be a great fit for the team. HR will send you an offer letter next week!
- YES, this screenplay is just what Bad Robot needs right now – I will talk to J.J. and set up a meeting next week!
- YES, you can count on my vote at the next Council meeting!

The NEW Elevator Pitch is designed to help you win, through a platform of persuasion. Are you prepared for "YES"?

Shortlink: http://bit.ly/sYgYwZ

The End of the Pitch is Only the Beginning

A key element of the NEW Elevator Pitch is realizing that the pitch does not end when you get a yes. That's when the real work begins.

STEP 7: YES! FINDING AGREEMENT

- You have to consider the implications of your elevator pitch. Every action has a 'ripple effect' – what's yours? Have you considered all the possible impacts, both good and bad? By considering the possibilities, you will build confidence in your pitch (and your responses, when your listener says, "Tell me more...")

- Assuming that your audience says, "YES," then: what happens for them? You have to anticipate the impacts your pitch will have on the audience in order to respond properly.

- But what happens to the organization if there's no agreement? You must demonstrate that you've thought this through, from a standpoint of both agreement and disagreement. What are the risks and/or pitfalls of taking a different path than the one you propose?

Success Criteria – Defining Victory

While you may not receive a job offer or a multi-million dollar investment out of your NEW Elevator Pitch, you have to measure your progress and define success using realistic terms. Ask yourself these questions:

- Am I closer to what I want?
- Have I proven that what I want is what's best for all of us?
- What's the next logical step?

In other words, you have to identify your "YES!" You have to prepare to win.

Believe It and You Just Might See It

Many of my clients and students have clearly invested their mental energy in preparing for the opposite of victory. Can you relate? "They won't like my pitch," our brains seem to tell us. "You will forget your key points," says the tape inside our mind. "Your voice sounds weird, and you're not very interesting," and the negative thoughts continue. Ever have any of those thoughts come into your head? (Me too!)

I'll never forget the time, as a young man, when I had to stand up in front of the whole school and perform a presentation. Ruled by fear, I talked myself out of whatever little talent I may have had at the time, and my terror caused my throat to close and my knees to shake. I was unable to make a decent sound! Catastrophe had struck, and I was powerless to stop it (or so I thought).

The embarrassment I felt that day has driven me to do what I do. Overcoming that adversity (it was totally self-inflicted!) makes me a better coach for my clients, and hopefully for you as well. You see, without understanding what it's like to be really afraid, I couldn't do what I do now. From nervous kid to national elevator pitch champion, I've run the gauntlet. I believe in life after death, not only for religious reasons, but because I've experienced it onstage...many, many times.

STEP 7: YES! FINDING AGREEMENT

Now I hope I can help you to avoid the mistakes that I've made, and believing in what's bad about yourself is the first thing you've got to reject. Here's how I turned things around: it started with changing my perspective.

Consider: everything has a front and a back. In other words, if what's bad is possible, then so is what's good. "No" and "Yes" are both available – how you pitch will make one more probable than the other. Which do you choose?

It's possible that you will succeed. It's possible that what you are saying can make a difference. It's possible that your audience wants to see you win, because victory for you means victory for others. You may not be the next Hillary Clinton, Ryan Reynolds or Jack Black in your presentation – so what? Are you interested in applause, or action? Results are your goal; keep your eye on what you need.

So many times, we only focus on the negative. Why? It's almost never completely fair, realistic or true – unless you want to design your pitch for abject failure. You owe it to yourself to consider success with equal measure. Every time you have a thought about pending disaster, balance it with equal airtime for thoughts about pending success. Envision yourself delivering the pitch that gets you the results you need. Prepare for what you want - and you just might find it.

PART I: SEVEN STEPS TO CLARITY

Permission to Succeed

In my coaching practice, I often have a recurring dialogue with clients. It goes something like this:

Client: Should I put my hands in my pockets during my pitch?

CW: Does that help you to make your point?

Client: Uh...well... [puts hands in pockets. Takes them out again] ...Well, it...

CW: When you watch yourself on video, does that gesture help your story, or hurt it?

Client: I think it hurts it. I'm trying to appear more relaxed but it kinda makes me look...disconnected. Or maybe just uncomfortable.

CW: [Silently agreeing] What would you like to do instead?

Client: I'd like to keep my hands out of my pockets, and gesture normally, like I do when I'm talking to my friends in my apartment.

CW: Then, why don't you do that instead?

Client: I'm just not comfortable with my [insert physical attribute here] and...

124

STEP 7: YES! FINDING AGREEMENT

CW: How would you present this material, if you were comfortable? What if you were comfortable with [physical attribute], and you were talking to your friends? I mean, how would you deliver your speech if you were totally cool with your [insert physical attribute here] and the whole situation. We've seen how you present when you believe that disaster is imminent... (it's hard to listen to someone in the middle of a tornado drill – especially when there's no tornado!) [laughter] What about how you would deliver your pitch if success is right around the corner? Why not make it like an acting assignment: do your pitch 'as if' you were thrilled with your [insert physical attribute here] and you were talking to friends. What would that feel like?

Your pitch would change if you would act as if success was headed your way. What stops us from giving the presentation we know we can? How legitimate are your concerns – or are you creating obstacles for yourself? What keeps you from using the gestures and inflection that would bring a new level of communication into our pitch is our inability to act as if success is right around the corner. "Oh," I can almost hear you thinking, "I'm not an actor. I can't do this 'act as if' thing..."

What!? We act 'as if' all the time! If you believe failure is the only option, you will act 'as if' there's no way to win. Similarly, if you believe that success is the only path, you will act 'as if' you can't lose! What distinguishes people of similar abilities is what they believe to be true about the world around them. Ordinary people become extraordinary because of what they believe to be true. Taking action on those beliefs is what delivers outstanding results – and outstanding elevator pitches. If you choose to act 'as if' you can be the presenter you need to be…. well, guess what? You will be – or at least, you will be closer to a great pitch. If you believe you have the skills to deliver a compelling elevator speech, you will begin to act 'as if' that's true. Still not convinced? Turn on the video camera, plug in a mental "as-if" that helps you, and see for yourself. You have the power to tell your story; why not let it out?

2:00 Your Two-Minute Drill
Permission Practice

You have, inside of you right now, the ability you need to deliver a great pitch. What's keeping you from giving yourself permission to win? Are you able to allow yourself to be the best presenter you possibly can – even if it means taking your hands out of your pockets?

How would you deliver your pitch if you were talking to your best friend? What would change for you? Give yourself permission to include those feelings – that attitude - in your pitch.

We've covered AUTHENTICITY before. Are you being true to yourself if you don't give yourself permission to be your very best?

STEP 7: YES! FINDING AGREEMENT

How would you deliver your pitch if you were the national elevator pitch champion? (I've met the guy, and believe me – his skills are not that much different than yours. In fact, he says he's been doing more with less his whole life! Maybe you have all the talents you need, to tell your story and focus on your listener. Do you – can you - believe that?)

• What would change for you if you knew your pitch couldn't fail, and that your audience could care less about [insert physical attribute here]? What if your message was the most important thing your listener would hear all day – how would you deliver your story?

The Secret of "YES!" – It's All About Permission

You already know how to have a good conversation. You do it all the time with your friends and your family. Even if you feel stilted or held back in your personal interactions, you know what a compelling conversation looks like. You can see it, hear it and identify it. We all have the ability to tell stories, and to persuade others at some level. All you have to do is give yourself permission to create the NEW Elevator Pitch. You can't transform into Ashton Kutcher, Natalie Portman or Ronald Reagan – and that's OK! Start where you are, and do what you can.

You can't change your voice, any more than you can change your height or your shoe size. But you can use your shoes, your height and your voice in a way that makes people say, "Tell Me More..." Don't try to be something you're not – it's not necessary. Learn to be more of who you are, and connect with the best possible presentation you can give. That presentation is based on connecting with your material, and connecting with your audience.

Put the "fun" into functional, and convey that enjoyment about your choices! *The NEW Elevator Pitch* doesn't go 'by the book' (which is why you can throw the other ones out, and delete them from your favorite e-reader – you've found the one you need! Ha!) The NEW Elevator Pitch is really about you writing your own story, and delivering it your way.

Shortlink: http://youtu.be/dEzUy37-dK8

Give yourself permission to access the energy you need (it's free, and it's already inside you). Assume interest on the part of your listener. Assume that your material is going to matter, and deliver your story as if it will make a difference – and it will. Give yourself permission to use the gestures that confirm your points (powerful gestures are free, readily available – and within your reach!) Give yourself permission to win, and get ready to hear a "YES!"

YOUR HIGHLIGHT REEL

- Give yourself permission to deliver your best elevator pitch – trust in the information you've gathered, and the exercises you have completed

- Act as if you are going to get what you want. Anticipate a "YES!" and overcome issues or obstacles along the path. Connect with your material in a powerful new way. You just might find what you're looking for, so be ready!

"YES!" is the final step in the process of CLARITY. You have the tools you need to find the story that's inside of you, right now. And you can deliver that message with purpose and persuasion, if you've followed the strategies in this book. Like any skill, preparation is the key. Take the time to watch yourself on video; you will learn more from observation than you can imagine. If you see a gesture that you don't like, why not change it? You're in the driver's seat. Take control of your story. You have the technology, you know the recipe – you have CLARITY on your side.

UNDER CONSTRUCTION

CLARITY: Step 7 is Yes!

Give yourself permission to finish your NEW Elevator Pitch with power. Put a really strong closing on your Pitch Paper – a closing that leads to the "YES!" you want. Act as if you are headed towards the exact outcome you expected, and convey a solution that gets a positive response.

What about speed networking? What do you do when the conversation is artificially shortened? The Two-Minute Drills have helped you to put together your story, and feel comfortable with the elements of your pitch. Now, let's put it all together and try a workout designed for a shortened pitch, in a speed networking session.

A Quick Guide to
Speed Networking

In a pinch for a quick pitch? Sometimes two minutes is too much – for your listener, or for your networking event. Here's a quick guide when the rules call for a more shortened and traditional pitch – using the concepts from the book.

Step 1: 10 seconds or less

Frame the conversation, using one of four conversation starters:

- "Have you ever noticed…?"
- "You know how…?"
- "I'll never forget the time when…"
- "Doesn't it seem like…?"

Make sure that your framing statement is something that is obvious and clear – something that almost anyone would agree with (because you want to start with a "yes", and a common frame of reference).

AVOID:

- Clichés
- Gimmicks

PART II: A QUICK GUIDE TO SPEED NETWORKING

- Being snarky or negative
- Opening with your name, rank and serial number. Introduce yourself AFTER you get out your first point

Step 2: 10-15 seconds

Connect to your key point, using an unexpected twist.

- The twist has to be honest and authentic
- The twist means an unexpected development or characteristic – something atypical about you, your company, or your idea – tied into your opening statement
- The twist further draws your listener in. Ideally, the response to the unexpected opening is, "Tell me more..."

Step 3: 20 seconds

What's your key theme, or message? What can you do with, through and for others?

- For any accomplishments, features or characteristics, ask yourself "So what?" at least three times
- Phrase all descriptions in terms of your listener. What can you/your product/your company do for the person right in front of you?

Step 4: 10 seconds

Consider the empty chair. Think about how your solution will affect your customer's customer, or other interested party who isn't in the room with you right now.

Step 5: 10 seconds

Close with an invitation. Invite your listener to take action, and participate in your solution in some way.

Finally, after you close with an invitation, be prepared for your audience to say, "Tell me more...." The new elevator pitch is a conversation, no matter how quick. This quick guide is merely a way to get the ball rolling.

What questions can you anticipate from your speed networking event, or other formal pitch practice? What questions do you hope you are asked? Prepare your answers carefully, as you engage in the rest of the conversation.

The Scenarios

These scenarios include tips from experts in the NEW Elevator Pitch, my own analysis, and model pitches, which I call "Perfect Pitch". Each scenario includes at least one exercise – a quick drill, designed to be accomplished in two minutes or less. The two-minute drill illustrates the key concept from the scenario, and gives you the means to take control and make changes in your message and your delivery. "The Breakdown" is a device for analyzing the elements of the pitch. In my coursework with executives and colleges, I break down the elevator pitch into seven sections – a sentence or two on each section, and you've got a perfect two minute pitch.

Even if these scenarios don't seem to apply directly to your situation, check them out anyway. Note that the names have been changed to protect the innocent; there are elements of fiction and "poetic license" within the factual concepts in the scenarios.

Read on to find out more from some folks who live and die by their elevator speech. Here are the scenarios that show you how to put the NEW Elevator Pitch into action.

Why Hire Me?

GET A JOB!

Use it when: you are being interviewed for a job and need to convince someone that you are the right candidate

"Why Hire Me" is a classic pitch, and one of the most important. Entire industries are devoted to making this story stick, but you will learn how to do it properly right here. Whether you are a Baby Boomer, Millennial or a Gen Xer, you need to master this NEW Elevator Pitch: your career depends on it.

The Millennial CEO

Five years ago, Dan Newman was a regional account manager for a Chicago-based manufacturer's representative, selling high-end electronics to small businesses. Today, just a few years later, he's the President and CEO at a multi-million dollar IT and integration firm. His ascent to the top office is especially impressive when you consider that he took the reins at a company he didn't start...all before his 30th birthday. Welcome to the "Why Hire Me?" pitch - courtesy of the Millennial CEO.

PART III: THE SCENARIOS

"Competence is the key to landing the job," Dan says, from his suburban Chicago office. Intense as you might expect, Dan is often quick with a joke (usually at his own expense) as we talk. A former college athlete and father of two, he explains that he has had to rely on his personal selling skills to build his track record.

But, what about when you don't have a track record?

How do you pitch, when your experience may not be exactly right for the role? After all, overcoming the issue of experience is the challenge for every job seeker – from Gen Y to the Silent Generation. You either have too much experience, or not enough – or it's in the wrong industry, or from an unknown company. How can someone overcome the challenge of experience?

Here's Dan's step-by-step process to pitching yourself as the perfect job candidate – and making your experience matter, when the stakes are high:

- **Confidence** – or more precisely, a "humble confidence". Dan explains that, no matter what your role or experience level, "The team has to believe that you can deliver value that they can't find somewhere else... If you don't believe in you, no one else will either."

- **Inspiration** – "A big part of my success has hinged on my ability to convince others that I can do what they need me to do. I refer to past accomplishments and experience, but – at the end of the day – people have to believe that you can get the job done." Transferring your beliefs to another is one of the hallmarks of inspiration, and a key to getting others to take action.

- **Results** – "It's all about packaging your accomplishments," according to Dan. Does your resume reflect your results, or just your skills? When you are asked for your elevator pitch, do you deliver those results in clear package for the interviewer?

- If a company is going to invest in you, you have to show that you really understand what they're trying to accomplish – and the implication of their challenge.

- **The Antidote for "Can't"** – "You have to remove the word 'can't' from your vocabulary," Dan says, without hesitation. "And you have to make sure the company understands and believes that –with you in place – that overcoming their challenge is now possible."

- **Delivery** – "What's the path to that profitability that all businesses seek?" Dan suggests that question as the centerpiece of any hiring strategy. In other words, what's the "Why?" from the hiring manager's perspective? You have to demonstrate that you understand how to deliver the results that are needed – even if those results are in engineering, customer service or cost accounting. Every role and every department has results; explain how your role would contribute to that accomplishment.

- **Go Beyond Your Experience** – What about new responsibilities – things you haven't got on your resume? "You have to show extraordinary competence in the area of your expertise – and then connect that track record to new opportunities and new challenges... Look at the experience you do have, and explain how it relates."

- **Leadership without Authority** – "If you want to move into a new role with new responsibility, you have to show how you've been able to marshal resources from diverse departments, without having an executive role." Leadership without a title is the first step towards getting one.

- **Research** – Know the company, and know your audience. "Do you know enough about me and my business," Dan asks matter-of-factly, "before you ask me to buy YOU?"

To find out more about Dan Newman, check out http://millennialceo.com. You can also check out his posts on the popular blog that he co-founded, http://www.12most.com

2:00 Your Two-Minute Drill

Injecting Confidence

The key to inspiring a hiring manager is to make your experience matter when the stakes are high. How do you do that, in two minutes or less? Start the timer, and answer the questions below:

Fill in the blanks:

- "The solution I can provide for this company is _____, and I'm different from the other applicants because _____. I've proved that quality time and time again, through my experience at _____."
- "I am at my best when _____."
- "My greatest professional accomplishment is _____."
- "One surprising thing you may not know about me is that I'm actually really good at _____."
- "The difference I believe I can make for your company is _____."
- "What's unique about my experience, as it relates to this position, is _____."

Focus

"Why Hire Me" is the pitch that really focuses on your listener. This speech is not about how badly you need the job, or how long you've been looking for an opportunity like this one, or ANYTHING other than what

139

PART III: THE SCENARIOS

YOU CAN DO FOR THE EMPLOYER. Focus on the difference you can make, and the solution you provide.

For the "Why Hire Me" pitch, it's critical that you invert and rearrange a key component of your elevator speech. As you know from previous chapters on the Langer study, the words "why" and "because" are a powerful way to make your point. In the job interview, you may be tempted to fall into this trap of Cause and Effect:

WHY... *Were you laid off, did you leave your last employer, were you let go, etc.*	BECAUSE... *(What you'd like to say)*
My division was downsized	My boss was a moron, and no one would listen to me
The company was shut down	The leadership team was a bunch of crooks and idiots
The industry shrank by more than 65%	And my manager was not smart enough to figure out how to keep me on board

These answers are extreme, to illustrate a point: haven't you ever felt this way before – that there was some blame that needed to be shared? Flip this chart for your

"Why Hire Me" pitch, and focus on making your experience meaningful to your prospective employer. After all, the sins of the past won't get you into heaven – and it doesn't serve you to describe the flaws of past bosses and companies. Focus on what you can do for the person in front of you, not on what's behind you.

Check out the flip side:

BECAUSE...	THAT'S WHY...
My division was downsized	*I came to understand the value of training, and I invested in additional MCSE certifications.*
The company was shut down	*Through the bankruptcy, I took action to make sure that the bankers and accountants had the information they needed, and I continued my diligence to the very end.*
The industry shrank by more than 65%	*That economic shift led me to develop three key presentations on cost-cutting and workforce realignment.*

2:00 Your Two-Minute Drill

Reverse Your Why

Time to set the timer! Fill in the blanks as you respond to this question:

"Why did you leave your last position?"
Answer for each of the companies on your resume.

Use the chart below.

BECAUSE... *(What was the business reason for change? Keep it simple and speak with CLARITY)*	THAT'S WHY... *(What did you do, learn, or demonstrate through the process, and how does it reflect on your VALUE to the potential employer)*

Pitch Perfect: Why Hire Me?

Example: How to Pitch to a Hiring Manager

Setting the Scene: Stephanie G. graduated at the top of her class at Cal-Poly San Luis Obispo, one of the top-ranked architecture schools in the country. She is interviewing for a San Diego-based architectural and engineering firm, with extensive ties to residential and commercial construction in Central America.

STEPHANIE: The greatest thing I learned about architecture? It didn't come from the classroom. My number one lesson came from an eight-year-old girl in Guatemala.

Last summer I worked on an international assignment for Habitat for Humanity. In Mixco [*the third-largest city in Guatemala*], I met Isabella. Isabella comes from a poor family, and she never thought she would ever have a house of her own. We used smart design concepts. We built four homes using all local resources. We held a big ceremony and gave Isabella her new home....actually, we

143

gave it to her parents, and of course [*laughs*] Isabella ran through the house right away. When she came out, she said to me in Spanish, "It all goes together!" It wasn't just about a roof over her head. It was about all the things under that roof, working together to create a functional space. She saw the things we take for granted for the first time. It was amazing.

Building that house required us to source items from within Guatemala. I'm fluent in Spanish, so I sourced most of the construction materials for Habitat. I also supervised a crew of about 20 for the framing and drywall.

In Guatemala, I found out that I'm at my best when I'm working with local resources. I like the challenge! My strengths are in communication, and I know now how to bring a design to life. I've already fought battles with electricians. I've had to re-draw the plumbing layouts! [*laughs*]

I still stay in touch with Isabella's family. I'm not sure she knows about the natural lighting or new attic insulation that we used. She understands that she has a space that's really *hers*. She has a place where she can learn, and grow, and create...other families do too. That's why I'm so interested in your expansion into Latin America. Are you looking for someone like me for your current projects in Guatemala?

THE BREAKDOWN

Here's a look at the elements of Stephanie's elevator speech, piece by piece. Note how she encapsulates her talents and her results in a memorable story – a story that is SO much more powerful than just a laundry list of accomplishments and characteristics! Also, note how the use of numbers and results has to be quantified in different ways for her work with Habitat. Stephanie uses a sincere emotional appeal to demonstrate a value that can't really be measured.

Elements of Stephanie's "Why Hire Me" Pitch

You may want to refer back to the speech to see the specific elements.

CAPTIVATE: Unexpected opening. The "Tell Me More…" is, "What did this little girl teach you?" "Why was that lesson more important than your school work?"

LANGUAGE: sets the scene.
Stephanie incorporates key words that are key strengths of hers. She knows these ideas are important to the firm:

- smart design concepts
- local resources
- scope of work (four homes)

PART III: THE SCENARIOS

AUTHENTICITY: Don't be afraid to laugh if something is funny. Be connected to your story!
Note the power of story and *emotional appeal.* Stephanie plays to her strengths (nurturing and coordination) plus her ability to work with people, without saying it directly. The story format is powerful AND memorable. She shows herself to be a keen observer of human nature with high "emotional intelligence".

RELEVANCE: the company is probably in need of a top architect, who is fluent in Spanish and can do these things. She also ties into her leadership abilities, and experience in managing others here.

INSPIRATION: show what matters to you, and make it matter to your listener. Architecture is about many things, but bringing designs to life is a central theme. She may not have all the experience in the world, but has some proven skills that could be very valuable!

TACT: She's the kind of person who follows up. She knows how to communicate effectively – *en español, tambien!*

YES! The answer is implied. After this passionate story, wouldn't you say, "YES!" to Stephanie? Or, at the very least, "Tell me more about your work in Guatemala…"

Knowledge breeds confidence; confidence conveys competence. Be knowledgeable, and humbly confident, to give yourself every opportunity to win that position with your NEW Elevator Pitch.

YOUR HIGHLIGHT REEL
Why Hire Me? Summary

- Show competence by elaborating on the accomplishments on your resume. Focus on what you can do for the company.
- Do your homework on the company, so you can show that you're paying attention
- Eliminate "Can't" from your vocabulary, and show the company how they CAN - with you in the role.
- Relate your experience to the position. Even if it's not an exact fit, turn to your track record of success.
- Use "why" and "because" as it relates to the solution you can provide, and consider reversing the order to focus on the effects of your past experience.

How to Pitch a TV Show

Use it when: you need funding for your creative venture - you are pulling together your message to pitch to a television network, producer, or artistic benefactor.

This is the mother of all elevator pitches. Well, not exactly: it's the mother, father and grandfather of all pitches, and it's often delivered by more than one person. As you may or may not know, the elevator pitch originally referred to creative types pitching their ideas to movie producers during an elevator ride. The idea of pitching a story in an elevator is a quaint idea from the past. The elevator platform has been replaced with the social platform, but when you want to get down to business, it's time to get face-to-face. No matter what your creative project, here's how to get your ideas produced.

So Many Pitches, so Few (Good) Shows

"I'm getting into a cab in New York City," David Poynter is saying. "And the cabbie asks me where I work.

SCENARIO: HOW TO PITCH A TV SHOW

When I tell him 'TNT, the cable network', he says, 'Do you know Ben Goldstin?' Well, yes I do, Mr. Cabdriver. Ben just happens to be my boss. Next thing I know, the cabbie is telling me about how Ben rode in his cab –over a year ago - and this guy pitched my boss on a great idea for a TV show. So before you can say La Guardia, this guy wants to tell me his pitch. He re-launches into his elevator speech for a TV Show- right there in the cab".

David Poynter is a Senior Manager for Current Programming at TNT. He provides creative oversight on four hit TV shows: "Rizzoli and Isles", "The Closer", "Falling Skies" and "Southland". Prior to TNT, he spent several years in development at the CW – where listening to TV-show pitches was virtually a daily event.

Here's what this production exec has to say about pitching a network studio:

Get in the Room - recommendations from a top agent or producer are needed, if you want to be taken seriously. "Of course, if J.J. Abrams [*Lost, Alias, Fringe, Star Trek*, etc.] has a new idea, we will definitely take a meeting. But for someone without a track record, relationships and recommendations are key."

"If you're serious about your pitch," Poynter says, "you have to get people in the room that want to hear what you have to say, and that can do something with your idea once you're done."

PART III: THE SCENARIOS

Show and Sell: Evidently, it's who you know in Hollywood, right? "Well, there's more to it than that. We've taken meetings – and bought shows from – students right out of USC film school. But they had an aggressive agent, and they worked hard to get in front of us with their idea. In the world of TV, it's all about the **execution** of the idea."

For the USC grads and their pitch, David says, "Those guys were pitching a soap about 20-somethings living in LA and trying to make their way in the world. Now, that's not an idea that anyone's going to go, 'Wow, we've gotta make this show'! But, these guys came in like bulldogs, and they had an agent from CAA that was all over it as well. These guys proved themselves to be very resourceful and capable by producing a 50-minute featurette. They pitched the show, and then said, "We produced this episode for you." It was unorthodox, but it demonstrated what they could do on a budget, and they did a great job – it really inspired confidence in green-lighting the idea."

Other visuals can also be useful in a TV show pitch. As David explains, "The CW bought a show; it was a mystery/adventure, with a supernatural hook. The story centered around this guy who came across a treasure trove of paintings in his grandfather's attic. He discovered that, within these paintings, there were clues to disastrous events - events that were going to happen in the future. The show was about trying to piece together the clues

150

based on elements in the paintings – and then averting the disaster once it was discovered. So, to help wrap our minds around the idea, the guys came in with mock-ups of 6-7 paintings, and they would show you, 'See this little clock beside the tree? That means this, and it leads the characters to this conclusion...'" Poynter explained that it's not common to use props during a pitch, but in this case, the pictures created a clear image and basis for the story line. (Ultimately, the network bought the script but did not produce the pilot – the show was #6 on a 5-show season pickup. But the pitch was still successful).

Point of Attack: you don't have to start at the beginning of the story. "If it's a character, if it's a guy like *House* (who we haven't seen on TV before), you don't want to start off with, 'Oh, it's a medical show, set in a hospital, blah blah blah...Immediately, you tune out: somebody pitching another medical show. Old news. Not interested. But, if you start with the *dialogue* of your guy – your lead character - reaming somebody out, telling somebody to 'Go die' ...and then, you find out he's a doctor at the hospital, you go, 'What'?!"

According to David, knowing where to start your tale is key to arresting the attention of your listener. "That's the difference between being a *storyteller*, and a *describer*" he says. (Which one are you?)

You Gotta Do Your Homework: Ultimately, it's all about knowing your audience. "If you're pitching to TNT, you have to understand our target market – the demographic is 25-54, and skews more female than male. You must demonstrate that you know the kinds of shows that we produce," David says.

"Given our demographics," Poynter says, "You shouldn't pitch a show about teenagers – take that to CW or ABC Family -- or a show that takes place on a space station in another galaxy – take that to SyFy – or a show with an antihero like Tony Soprano – take that to pay cable, cause at TNT we do shows about everyman-like heroes and heroines. Or a musical – take that, well, just somewhere else. TNT isn't doing musicals. You gotta know this stuff coming in."

Creating Your Pitch

Assuming that you've got the connections to get in the room, the ability to execute, and the research you need about the network, here's David's advice for a pitch that would make him say, "Tell Me More…"
Creative Pitch Strategies

1. Paint a vivid, clear picture of your story, your characters, and your dialogue

2. Make it emotional and relevant to the people in the room

3. Immediately make your story compelling by assuming the person you are pitching to **is** your audience (the viewer at home)

4. Consider your "triggers" – what is going to arrest the attention of the viewer? "You can arrest their attention with something that is going to visually get their mind active and engaged," David says.

   - *Lost* is a great example – imagine starting your pitch with the opening plane crash – that image, that sequence, has become an instant classic for anyone who's seen it. "The plane crash is so visual, so compelling that you are immediately pulled in. If you've got 'em, then you can take 'em anywhere you want."

5. Make it personal, to yourself, and to your audience, Poynter says. For example, "Let's say you used to be a lawyer, and you're pitching a legal show, you should lead off with your personal connection to the legal profession. Start conversationally, and personally. Then, you're not talking to someone who's judging you – you're talking directly to the people who are there in the room." Building rapport is always important - when you get people engaged, that's the first step to getting people on your side.

To find out more about the latest lineup on TNT, check out http://www.tnt.tv.

2:00 Your Two-Minute Drill

Find a friend or a coach, and see what you can come up with, using some Hollywood lessons for improving your pitch. Set the timer, and get your creative juices flowing!

1. **Think of a different 'point of attack' in your story**. Start off your pitch by talking about the future – what has happened as a result of your initiative? Maybe your new business idea leads to greater energy efficiency, or smaller Bluetooth devices, or faster service at the BMV (we could all use some of that!). Think like JJ Abrams: what timeline would serve your story best? (You currently have two minutes to come up with your answer!)

2. **Change your hook:** What's the most compelling element of your pitch? Have you really considered that one element that will "arrest" your listener, as David suggests? How many can you come up with, in less than two minutes?

Pitch Perfect:
Why Should I Produce
Your Project?

Example: Pitching a TV Show

Our scene unfolds near the Farmers' Market in Los Angeles. Seated near the pool table at Lola's on Fairfax, two CBS development execs are listening to Delk Rivers, a writer with an idea for a new TV show. Rivers is 31, and his writing credits include the cancelled NBC series, *Chase*, and six episodes of *CSI: Miami*. On his left sits Shane Deegan, a veteran writer of over 30 episodes of *NCIS: Los Angeles* and a co-producer on that show. Delk begins the pitch, as Shane and the CBS executives listen...

DELK: So, here's how we start. There's a beautiful woman, in a tracksuit. She's in the ladies room at a high-end restaurant, maybe it's a country club, and she's looking in the mirror. Two thugs in suits bust into the girl's john. Your grandma comes out of the first stall. She sees the two guys, freaks out, screams, and runs out of the bathroom.

PART III: THE SCENARIOS

SHANE: There are two guys. Two handguns. One big problem. But the babe with the lipstick stays put, right?

DELK: That's right. The guy with the thicker neck says, "We need the canister, Agent. Now," while the other guy "CHK-CHK" chambers a bullet in his 9mm pistol.

The agent stays cool. She looks at them in the mirror. Wipes a smudge from her lipstick. To the mirror, she sighs and rolls her eyes, "You fellas are gonna have to take it from me."

What happens next is the hairiest fight scene since "Kill Bill". The beautiful agent, still looking at the mirror, pushes on the sink and kicks both of these poor bastards at the same time. The guy on the left crashes into the bathroom door and falls into the bathroom stall. The other guy has dropped his gun, but he recovers quickly. Instantly he grabs her and is rewarded with an elbow in the gut and a heel in his groin. He quickly kneels to pray with his hands on his mashup. Quick cut to her right wrist, as a blackjack comes down out of her sleeve and into her clenched fist. This agent is instantly armed and even more dangerous. The fight proceeds, until the director yells, "CUT!"

SHANE: The cameras pull back, to reveal the set of *NCIS: Los Angeles*. There's Daniela Ruah (*she plays Agent Blye on the show*) coming up to hug the "agent" and tell her "Great job!" LL Cool J helps one of the thugs to get up off of the floor, as we see the title graphics come into view: "SO YOU WANNA BE A STUNTMAN".

DELK: SO YOU WANNA BE A STUNTMAN is the latest reality series from CBS. It has all the components of a reality/game show, like *Survivor*, combined with some of the wildest stunts you can imagine. There's also a promotional tie-in to the top shows, like *The Mentalist*, *NCIS*, and *Hawaii 5-0*. In this case, the contestants compete for roles on the top CBS shows, and work on set with some of the great "names" in the business. Contestants go "behind the scenes" with top stunt coaches and celebrity guests, who show them how to "sell" a fight.

DELK: Make it to the finals, and you get a part on one of the new shows for next season. Shane is here to tell you more about some of the tie-ins with NCIS and some possible ideas for our panel of judges.

THE BREAKDOWN
Pitching as a Team

Two pitchmen, one story. Notice how each plays a part in the tale, and they play off of each other. Shane asks, "Right?" even though he knows what happens next – it's a small touch to show the connection between the storytellers. And Delk throws it back to Shane, there at the end, leaving the *NCIS* expert to tell his portion of the story as part of the built-in "Tell Me More..."

PART III: THE SCENARIOS

These two professional storytellers come together to do what they do best: tell a story that hooks the listener, of course, but tell a story *that's built to sell*. Consider several formidable hooks in this pitch:

- Viability: *NCIS Los Angeles* is already at the table. Shane, a producer on *NCIS*, has joined Delk for the pitch. There are two writers with major television credits pitching the idea.

- Marketing appeal: Note the opportunity to feature actors and shows on the reality series. What's the value of those tie-ins to CBS' promotional strategies? If cross-promotion is desirable, it looks like this show could deliver the goods.

- Perceived Value: CBS knows the value of hit reality TV. Shows like *The Amazing Race, Survivor* and *American Idol* are major network franchises for CBS and elsewhere.

However, this pitch is not foolproof. There are several loose ends – a handful of "Tell Me More..." questions that could stall this elevator on the first floor.

For example, what about the production costs? Where do these "stunt people" come from – do they audition, like "American Idol"? No, that won't work. You can't jump off the couch and onto the set of a network TV show where you're fake fighting in an exploding building. Would this show be a "big break" for the contestants, or really just another gig for working stuntmen and women? Hard to know for sure right now, but that's all to be discussed if (and when) the studio says, "Tell Me More…"

You may never pitch a television series, but there will be many instances in which you and your team are pitching a project or an idea. Little connections in the story can make the back-and-forth seem as natural as your next breath. Your pitch has to have a strong dynamic between you and your partners and have viability, marketing appeal, and perceived value.

Use the techniques of a TV pitchman to get support for any creative project you might have. Develop attention-grabbing visuals that demonstrate your expertise, know your audience and refine your hook. If you can successfully pitch a TV show, you can pitch anything.

YOUR HIGHLIGHT REEL
Advancing Your Creative Project
For a TV Show or Otherwise:

- Get in the room
- Demonstrate your competence
- Show and sell
- Grab the attention of the listener with a startling point of attack
- Do your homework

How to Pitch to Angel Investors

Use it when: you are seeking additional sources of funding for your business concept, organization or idea, or when you are launching a start-up. Useful for pitching with a team, to a team of investors.

Pitching investors is a tough sell. These guys have heard it all – twice. What they haven't heard is the NEW Elevator Pitch. While the following scenario deals with raising money from angel investors, you can use this pitch to approach others in the financial community or financial decision makers in your own company.

Inspired by Guy Kawasaki's *The Art of the Start*, I quickly realized that entrepreneurs are looking for ways to reach the financial markets. Perhaps that last sentence describes your situation; an investor pitch is one of the most essential. You have to be able to get in the room, and get your story across, or you're never going to see your idea come to life.

SCENARIO: HOW TO PITCH TO ANGEL INVESTORS

 Combined with my work coaching new ventures, and my involvement with the Entrepreneurship Series at the University of Texas at Dallas, I'm committed to helping entrepreneurs conquer the Shark Tank. I've developed some guidelines and anecdotes designed to help you to find the funding you need, but there's still more to the story. If you're interested in learning more about how to reach investors with a pitch that yields results, check out http://theinvestorpitch.com, or just fire up that QR code on your smartphone. The website includes videos, exercises and courses specifically designed for the day you talk to the Angels, VCs or other folks that can help you to launch your idea. In the meantime, I wanted to share some of my favorite anecdotes, from some of my favorite people, to help you to make sure you have the right perspective before you meet with the Angels.

Harry's World:
Impeccably dressed in a suit and tie, Harry Elkin is the guy who makes a pocket square make sense. Looking younger than his years, with a quick with a grin and a handshake for everyone, Harry is a master networker within the financial community. A veteran of multiple pitches to venture capitalists, investors and venture capital firms, he has spearheaded technology startups and business development efforts across multiple industries.

PART III: THE SCENARIOS

Here's the view from Harry's world, on how to say it and sell it to an angel investor:

- **Pitch your people not your ideas** – "There's no shortage of cool ideas," Harry says, from booth number three at his favorite North Dallas hangout. "People never invest in cool technology – investors invest in *people*. They invest in the people that can turn an idea into revenues." That's why the best pitches come from the folks who are surrounded by the best people – including a successful, seasoned Board of Advisors. For the Angels, the question isn't "What have you got" but "Who have you got?" Harry continues, "Before your pitch begins, people need to know the experience base of the team. Who's surrounding your idea, to make sure it will succeed?"

Other Viewpoints:

Internet entrepreneur Trey Bowles agrees with Harry on the importance of "who". Trey has significant experience with building and running technology based media companies, beginning in 2001 when he helped build one of the fastest-growing companies in the history of the Internet age — Morpheus – that had over 100 million application downloads in less than one year. Trey advises, "Use the word 'we' in describing any accomplishment; even if you made it happen, the execution and delivery of anything of value always involves the help of others. Pitching with 'I, me, my' gives a clear indication of your management style…and it's not a good one."

SCENARIO: HOW TO PITCH TO ANGEL INVESTORS

Dallas angel investor John Antos is co-author on three books on advanced financial accounting – he knows the numbers, but he focuses on people. He's a veteran of over 500 pitches, and his company, Value Creation Group, Inc., has multiple investments in various new technology businesses. "When it comes to a pitch, I always ask, 'Who's the jockey?' In other words, who's in charge, because a good jockey (with even a mediocre idea) always trumps a great idea with a lousy jockey!"

- **How are you protected from the Big Gorillas?** – What is to keep Apple, or IBM, or Smith Kline, or Black and Decker, or whoever else, from entering your market space? If the market space is attractive to you, what's to keep a better-financed existing business from coming into your territory? Show that you've thought about the other guys, and you've got a solution that can stand up against gorilla-sized competition.

- **Present reasonable financials** – "What you need to establish are your ASSUMPTIONS," Harry explains. "Truth be told, investors never expect your numbers to be correct. They expect the numbers to be wrong 100% of the time." Investors seek 'reasonableness', according to Harry – and so, you absolutely must provide a detailed workbook with pro-formas, based on reasonable assumptions.

Angel investor John Antos agrees. "We seek out details on other companies that have sold in the same industry, and we have a formula for evaluation. If your projections or expectations

163

are out of line with what the market has done with similar organizations, well, you just might be making a wild pitch." Story and assumptions are your trump cards, in an Angel pitch.

- **Consider Targeting a New Industry** – Many Angels don't want to invest in businesses that have already been successful- they are seeking to diversify their portfolio. "If you're going to pitch telecom to a guy who's been in the telecom space, he typically will know more about that industry than you do," Harry says, speaking from experience. "As a result he's going to be inclined to show his technical knowledge in a way that can point out the chink in your armor. He could ask questions in front of a number of investors that you can't answer in a meaningful way. He could be the one naysayer that could derail your whole effort. So, in many cases, it's better to have an audience that is more sensitive to an entrepreneur's plight and willing to invest in new ideas."

"Get out of your normal comfort zone," John Antos says, gesturing at a copy of 'Futurist' magazine. "I may not be immediately concerned with how we might derive energy sources from the moon, like this cover story says here, but I take the time to read and consider new viewpoints. As entrepreneurs and investors, we have to be open to new ideas if we are going to find the next big thing."

- **Pick your best pitchman (or woman)** – "An entrepreneur needs someone who can articulate why a solution makes sense, why this idea is directionally correct right now," Harry says emphatically. Many times, the best person for the storytelling job is not the one who came up with the original idea. Finding the best communicator is the key to showing how you can build a team - *especially* with the Angels. Harry describes it this way: "It's a selfless act to allow others to play to their strengths, and it shows the entrepreneur's foresight in building a team. Technical expertise can be a liability in a pitch meeting, if you can't explain your idea in a way that a layman can understand." Harry continues, "Cool technology, explained by a technology guy, is often confusing. ... Often times – and I hate to say this – but, often times [the technology guys] are the worst ones to give the pitch."

- **Don't Pitch the Market** – "If you say, 'The market size is $2Billion and we plan on capturing 0.01% of this market', bang! you lose," Harry says, taking a sip from a cup of coffee. "Investors want reasonable ideas on why you are going to succeed in a crowded market – it doesn't matter how big it is. You will hear very quickly that you have to build your revenue model from the ground up. You have to say, 'I will build this many units, I will sell this many units, year 1, 2, 3 - and here's why'." Focusing on your particular strengths – and your specific efforts – is more compelling than the size of the market.

PART III: THE SCENARIOS

- **Questions are the Key** – "If your audience isn't asking questions, then you've lost them," Harry says. "Meeting at your place? That's how you know when your pitch succeeds with the angels."

According to Trey Bowles, you have to be willing to answer tough questions from potential investors. If you "duck"or get defensive, you arouse suspicion, anger, or both. "After you explain your business concept, expect to get some questions. It may be self-evident to you what your new technology does, but that doesn't mean it's crystal clear to your potential benefactors. No matter what, don't get angry! Keep your cool when investors tell you there's some stuff they don't understand. Don't say, 'You just don't get it!' ...because that's exactly what I'll say when you ask for my money!"

`2:00` Your Two-Minute Drills

Welcome to a series of three Two-Minute Drills to help you get ready for that pitch to the angels. More exercises and detailed instruction is available at http://theinvestorpitch.com

Drill #1: Build Your Team

In one minute or lessor write a brief, one-sentence bio for the five key members of your team.

Now in one minute, explain how the experience of each team member will contribute to the success of your new enterprise.

SCENARIO: HOW TO PITCH TO ANGEL INVESTORS

Drill #2: The Antidote for Egomania

> Who else could give your business pitch to the Angels? Write down every reason why someone else – your business development person, your CFO, whoever – is better qualified to give this pitch than you are.

Drill #3: Tech Check

> Speak to your rabbi, or the woman at the dry cleaners, or one of your daughter's college-age friends, and deliver your two-minute pitch. Explain that you are looking for third-party feedback, to make sure that your business concept is clear and concise. When you finish your pitch, ask them to explain what it is that you do. Two great questions to use, when soliciting feedback: "What did you like best?" "What would you like to know more about?" Look for clues regarding:

- Concepts that are too technical for someone outside of your industry to convey, in their reply.

- Similar responses on what the listener would like to know more about. In a good pitch, you should be able to predict the "Tell me more..." questions – are you able to guide your listener to the response you want?

- Gather fresh perspectives – if you've been working for months or years to bring your product to market, you may be too close to it to pitch it effectively. Excellent advice can often come when you least expect it, so make sure you practice informally with folks (not family members!) that can help show you what you haven't seen so far.

Pitch Perfect: Why Should I Invest in Your Company?

Example: How to Pitch to Angel Investors

Introducing Aviza, a design and manufacturing company:

> Here's a brief overview of this fictional organization:
>
> *Aviza is a fashion design company specializing in innovative sports eyewear solutions for triathletes, marathon runners, and fitness enthusiasts. And unlike Oakley, Ray Ban or Maui Jim, our products are built to go from glasses to swim goggles to prescription lenses with just a click. One pair, three sports: so triathletes can shift from running to swimming to cycling in a matter of seconds.*

Carlos Mendes is the Director of Business Development for Aviza Eyewear. The company has received a small six-figure investment from friends and family, allowing them to fund design and prototype development for a unique brand of sport sunglasses. The

169

PART III: THE SCENARIOS

team has secured low-cost offshore manufacturing for their innovative designs, but they need more capital to produce the product in mass quantities. Carlos, Linda Sifuentes (the CEO and lead designer) and Jeff McDonald (Operations) are pitching a group of investors in Miami. Carlos stands up and moves to the front of the room as he speaks. [Note: Luxottica bought Sunglass Hut in 2007]

CARLOS: When Linda [the CEO] first told me about Aviza, my first reaction – quite frankly – was, 'this will never work!' The market is too crowded. Sunglass Hut owns the market. If you're not with Luxottica, you're not in Sunglass Hut. You are nowhere. So I said to Linda, 'How are you going to get into Luxottica with a new brand?' and she said, 'Stop. Stop. STOP. That's my line. How are YOU going to get into Luxottica with a new brand?' [the group laughs].

Jeff [Operations Manager] and I spent 12 years at Sunglass Hut, and we survived the acquisition in '07, so we still have a lot of friends there. Soooo…. 12 days ago, we got a signed letter of intent from Sunglass Hut. If we can produce the Aviza in sufficient quantities, Luxottica will put us in half of their US stores. So, that's 781 stores right there – plus online sales. Hm. So I said, OK…Then, I thought about it some more, and I thought this still isn't going to fly. How can you get a foothold against Ray Ban, or Oakley? I mean, Luxottica owns Oakley – wouldn't they favor their own brand? But Jeff, our Operations Manager, stepped me through the unique advantages of

Aviza – which we'll talk about more in a few minutes. Basically, Sunglass Hut wanted to know, what's beyond Oakley? And we showed them a solution. They liked it, but I still wasn't convinced. I mean, look at consumer spending right now! Look at other retail plays – even Luxottica is down by x% this morning! How are we going to get traction while consumer confidence is so low?

Well, I can't change the market. There's no way I can bump up consumer spending, and neither can you. I mean, maybe if we all go down to the Aventura Mall today...but that won't help the whole country. [mild chuckles, since two of the angels live in Aventura.] But we thought about it, and if we create a world-class product with unique advantages to the ultra-sports enthusiast, the upside on this venture gets very, very attractive. We've created the prototypes and sold the concept to the major distributor for eyewear. Now, we're seeking a $2.1 million investment to fund operations and manufacturing, through our facility in Venezuela. The deal book will show you the financials and our assumptions, but before we go there – let's try on some new sunglasses, and see how Aviza really fits for you.

THE BREAKDOWN

Here's a look at the elements of Carlos's elevator speech, piece by piece. Carlos absolutely connects with his opening remarks, because he says what everyone is thinking: "This will never work!" But, if it does, the upside could be huge. Would you have the courage to speak honestly and openly, the way Carlos does? Could you begin with what every investor is thinking, and be candid and forthright...and STILL sell your idea? You can, if you really trust in your concept and your team.

Think about it: An investor only needs one really good reason to invest. Carlos doesn't waste time trying to sell 16 benefits (or 23 retail chains) to this group. Once he's established a connection, he moves to a clear and precise call to action, with a dollar amount for the investors to consider. See below....

CAPTIVATE: In this case, the "This will never work" opening is completely unexpected because it's as if he's reading the investors' minds. How *will* this thing get off the ground? The answer lies in Carlos' ability to layout the team's solution for the audience. His opening demonstrates some of the rapport among the team.

LANGUAGE- Carlos establishes a surprising level of credibility:

- He knows the "threat" (in this case, retail distribution through Sunglass hut)

- He worked for the threat – implying intimate knowledge of the market, and the market challenges

How does this perspective inspire confidence for the Angels? The team (although it was probably him, primarily) has already conquered the threat. The investors will certainly drill into the history of the team, as part of their due diligence. But that comes later - the "we" language is important here, as Carols has a "Who" that's very powerful, indeed.

AUTHENTICITY: Drilling further into a contrarian process, Carlos is speaking the thoughts of the investors, via a logical and clear-headed approach to the industry. The interest shown by Sunglass Hut indicates that their product is both timely and interesting (Carlos' "Tell me more..." is: Why are they interested in looking beyond Oakley? Could it be that the brand has peaked, or is in decline?) Wouldn't you like to know?

RELEVANCE: Continuing with the third and final obstacle, Carlos shows that he knows the group, and establishes a familiarity through a humorous interjection. Perhaps the most relevant part of an angel pitch is the current state of the market. If conditions are favorable, then results can be managed to greater success. How do you pitch in a tough economy? By acknowledgement, and demonstrating a clear path to success. But that level of detail comes later...

INSPIRATION: Comes when the obstacles are overcome, minimized or (at the very least) identified (the talk about consumer spending and market conditions). The upside is the "why" for the angels. The upside has to be shown to be compelling, but not over-sold.

PART III: THE SCENARIOS

TACT: The direct approach. The number is $2.1 million. The upside is real, and powerful, but not detailed (that's a "Tell me more…" answered in detail in the deal book, which he hasn't handed out yet). Carlos says exactly what he needs. The focus here is on getting the Angels to buy in to the concept and the team. Without that connection, the numbers and financials won't mean much. Remember, this pitch involves the Angels – the personal connection is important here.

YES! Now is the time to pass out the deal books, and let the investors get a look at the numbers and the assumptions. The "Tell Me More…" should be focused on the upside – BECAUSE THAT'S WHAT HE LEFT OUT OF THE PITCH. What about other retail outlets for sunglasses, such as sporting goods stores? Won't they carry the products as well?

Ah yes! You are picking up what Carlos is laying down…. Wouldn't it be great if the investors asked those questions? Clearly, Carlos has thought about the outcomes he wants, and the questions that will get him there.

Whether you are pitching a business proposal to a banker, a Vice President at a Silicon Valley VC, or an Angel, you need to come across as confident, reasonable, and committed. How will you convey, "I've thought this through"? Or even better, "We've thought this through", in your pitch?

YOUR HIGHLIGHT REEL
Invest In My Company - Pitching to the Angels

- Pitch your people, not your ideas
- Watch out for big competitors
- Prepare complete and reasonable financials
- Choose the right person to make the pitch
- Don't pitch the market, pitch your *assumptions*
- Answer questions with calm enthusiasm, and prepare for the questions you'd most like to hear

The Informal Networking Pitch

Use it when: You want to meet new people in a professional context, such as a coffee shop or cocktail party. You are doing business development; you want to expand your personal/professional network

Casual conversations aren't really that casual when you can use them to collect contact information that is valuable for your business. This NEW Elevator Pitch will help you expand your business as you run errands, take your kids to events or just get a cup of coffee.

The Networking Pitch

"People *don't* want to talk to me," Joe Nemmers explains. A compact and athletic father of two boys, Joe is one of the most easygoing and amiable people I've ever met – and an expert on how to deliver an informal pitch. Nobody wants to talk to you? Say it ain't so, Joe!

"It's because", Joe says, "I'm a *realtor*."

SCENARIO: THE INFORMAL NETWORKING PITCH

According to Joe, the most hated professions for the last 20 years are (in order):

1. Lawyers
2. Car Salesmen
3. **Realtors**

"You know why lawyers are number one?" He deadpans, "Because they hang out with a lot of realtors!"

This challenge is common, for anyone whose business depends on networking. You have to develop an informal pitch that makes a connection with the listener without alienating them. If your listener senses that your informal pitch is shifting to a sales pitch, they will never say, "Tell me more…"

"People don't want to talk to realtors, because they don't want to get hustled. Right or wrong, people are not crazy about realtors", Joe says. "But my business depends on referrals and networking, and so I've had to develop my own strategy for telling my story. I call it 'The Starbucks Speech'".

"The Starbucks Speech"
Picture yourself in line at your favorite coffee establishment. Perhaps there's someone you'd like to meet – someone who could potentially become a client for your business. Looks like the NEW Elevator Pitch is about to get a latte…

PART III: THE SCENARIOS

"By the time [your contact] gets to the counter to order their drink," Joe explains, "they're gonna be thinking about what they want in their cappuccino, so you gotta catch 'em before they order their drink."

Find a way to engage- quickly: "Say hello, notice the surroundings. Comment on something that you see in a newspaper headline. Maybe [your contact] is in running gear, and I'll say, "So how was your run? I feel guilty that I'm not out there!" Just anything to initiate the conversation."

Know Your Audience: Some people are ready and willing to talk, and some people aren't. "Some folks aren't in a social mood – but maybe that's just caffeine withdrawal, in either case, you just have to bail out," Joe explains. "But just making a friendly comment can start a conversation. Some folks aren't interested in having a chat – so, I watch for body language: going to their phone, fidgeting in their purse, stepping closer to the counter. Those moves are usually a pretty good indication that they don't want me invading their space."

Have an Objective: "My goal, beyond just being friendly, is to create an exchange of information. I want to get my business card in their hand, and – my ideal – is to get their email address or some way to connect with them. I don't jump to 'what do you do' – that's too common. If the person is professional, I might ask, 'So are you getting some coffee to take to work? That's what I'm doing'. I don't want people to feel like I'm trying to pull information out of them; it has to be a conversation.

"If you ask a question, get a response, and you have a follow-up question – you've created that conversation."

Expect the "Tell Me More…": "I don't let the conversation go, until I establish what I do. Because once I establish what I do, I'm confident that they are going to ask me one of three questions:

1. How's the market?
2. How's your business?
3. What's your neighborhood/area specialty?

Does it work?
All the time.

"One client," Joe says, "she never gave me her information, but at the end of our conversation I pulled out my business card. 'Don't know if you might be in the market for buying or selling a home', I said, 'but if you or someone you know is looking for a realtor, I'd love to have a conversation with you at some point.' By that time, we were at the register and it was over. She ordered her coffee, her phone was ringing, and she was gone.

"One week later, my phone rang. It was her, and we started the dialogue about finding a lease property for her family."

PART III: THE SCENARIOS

Have Something Different to Add to the Conversation: In addition to being a realtor, Joe Nemmers is also one of the most well-known and hard-working actors in the Dallas/Fort Worth area. "Being an actor is a big help to my pitch. People may see me on a commercial, or a TV show - or they may have never seen me before. Either way, I try to talk about it – because being an actor is interesting to people. Folks may not always ask me about being in real estate, but 100% of the time, people will always ask me about being an actor."

Facebook is Big: Being on Facebook is crucial, according to Joe. "People feel good about doing business with people they know. It's important for my clients to see my kids, see my posts, and see what I'm about. Being seen online, checking out a profile in a kind of informal setting, helps accelerate the conversation. Now, more people reach out to me on Facebook. I get more connections on my profile than I do via email." So, in order to get people to like you, you have to get people to "like" you. (What's your presence, dear reader, on the social platform – and how does it help deliver your pitch online?)

Accelerators: You really have very little time, so here are the three keys to the Starbucks speech, according to Joe:

1. **You have to be real, and engage in real conversation.** Any business relationship starts with a genuine interest in the other person

2. **Courage:** "If you don't start a conversation, there's no conversation to end," Joe says, simply. No risk, no reward – you have to reach out and make the connection.

3. **Find a way to follow-up:** " Suggest that you connect on Facebook, and give 'em your card," Joe says, and by way of example, "'Would you mind if I followed up with you, with some information on the current market, or real estate, or something that offers some value (and service)?' Some will say 'yes', just to be polite, but you never know who may need your services one day."

What About Rejection?

"I don't take it personally," Joe says. "People, for the most part, aren't saying no to me because of me (unless I'm uncomfortable with my message). They simply don't have a need for what I have to offer. That's different than who I am. You have to change your thinking from how many people tell you 'no' vs. how many people tell you 'yes'. Any time you're trying to establish a business relationship, people respond to confidence more than anything else. Confidence establishes credibility, and credibility establishes trust. If you're speaking to someone with the expectation or fear that they are going to say 'no', you aren't going to come across as confident. But, if you speak to them as if your expectation that the audience will say 'yes', your confidence and your results will increase."

PART III: THE SCENARIOS

What's the best way to improve your confidence? Have a plan, and practice, practice, practice - starting right now. Check out your two-minute drill on the next page.

`2:00` Your Two-Minute Drill

At a coffeehouse of your choosing, start a conversation with a stranger, before he or she orders their coffee. In this drill, each step counts as a certain number of points (in parentheses). See if you can get all 10 points.

- Engage with them, based on the surroundings, to start a conversation (+1)
- Find out what they do for a living (+2)
- Get their contact information (+3)
- Agee to connect on Facebook, LinkedIn, or some other social network (+1)
- Give them one of your business cards (+3)

How did you do? Your score: _____

Extra Credit: Offer to buy your new friend's coffee, and explain what you are trying to do an exercise from the wildly entertaining and eye-opening new book, *The NEW Elevator Pitch*. When they say, "Tell Me More..." be sure to give them the website. If they contact us, we'll give you a surprise!

Pitch Perfect:
The Informal Pitch

Example: Coffee Talk

Setting the Scene: A busy coffee shop, 7:45am. Two well-dressed businessmen are waiting in line for their favorite morning beverage. Both are carrying Chicago Tribune newspapers while they wait. The coffee shop is a high-tech haven, bustling with people seeking their caffeine fix. At the tables, it seems like everyone is peering into some kind of smartphone or computer tablet. One business man, named Terry, turns to the other and says:

TERRY: I think we're the only ones in here without a tablet PC.
[*pauses to look around the coffee shop at all the hubbub of activity*]

When I look around I always feel like I must be missing something, but I still like to be able to touch the news [*Folds newspaper under his arm*]. I guess you must feel the same way? [*As his listener looks at his own newspaper and shrugs, with a look that says, 'Guilty as charged'*]. Old school, I guess.

You know what I mean? I work for [*a residential real estate firm in Chicago's NW suburbs*]. I help some of our neighbors buy and sell properties around here. That's not an easy gig in this economy, even here in Barrington Hills.

The Other Guy: You're in real estate?   How's the market right now?

TERRY: [*Leans in for emphasis*] Lately I've been seeing a lot of traffic in West Dundee. [*Coffee guy leans back, raises his eyebrows.   He looks skeptical.   Surprised, even*]. I know, right? But that's where the market is right now. I tweet a lot about those listings, the ones outside of Barrington Hills. Believe it or not, I get a lot of inquiries from twitter. You'd be surprised, some of my properties in West Dundee rival what you see in Barrington Hills! They're newer, more affordable, but similar size and amenities. You may not have the same 24 hour gated entry. [*He pauses for emphasis*] You also don't have the same tax burden, either. There are differences, but not inside the home. I just sold Larry Bangler's place [*a well-known local executive at Motorola*] in Barrington Hills, because I've been working this city since the late '80's. My reputation is why Larry chose me. But that sale wasn't easy. Still, we got it done in less than 100 days. That's about 156 days better than the average. It wasn't a fire sale, either. [*Looks around at the multitude of tablet PCs*] Some people let technology rule their lives, but for me tech is just a tool. A handshake still matters to me and my clients. My name is Terry Mathers [*extends hand*] – if you ever thought about selling your house I hope you'd keep me in mind. Maybe we could connect on linked in, or Facebook? Or how about an old-fashioned business card – that would go great with my newspaper!

When delivering an informal networking pitch, remember to find someone who is approachable and open to conversation. Begin your pitch with a friendly greeting and engage them in conversation. Have a goal for your contact, and if you succeed in attaining that goal, give yourself a prize, a free refill!

YOUR HIGHLIGHT REEL
The Informal Pitch

- Find a way to engage quickly
- Make sure your audience is in the mood to talk
- Have an objective in mind
- Expect the tell me more
- Use social media to develop your connection

Asking for a Raise

Use it when: You need to bring some expert negotiating skills to the NEW Elevator Pitch. This pitch can help move your career forward – or, at the very least, improve your paycheck.

This is a challenging NEW Elevator Pitch. When you give this pitch, you have to be aware of the fact that you may want a very different outcome from the person you are pitching. Knowing when and how to ask for a raise is one of the most important pitching skills you will ever learn.

Relevance is the Key

While there's no magic formula for getting a raise, the NEW Elevator Pitch gives you the perfect format for building your business case.

The best way to phrase your request is in terms of your value to the organization, not the organization's value to you. In other words, your personal financial situation is not relevant – your bills, obligations, etc. are not the company's responsibility.

SCENARIO: ASKING FOR A RAISE

Asking for a raise is the ultimate test in creating relevance. One party is very interested (the employee), the other (the company), not so much. So many employees will phrase their pitch in terms of what matters to them, instead of considering their value (relevance) to the company.

Your NEW Elevator Pitch for a raise must:
- Explain what you have done for the company in a way that inspires agreement from your boss.

- Specify what you will do for the company (after all, the organization will need to know what kind of results it will be buying)

- Reflect the company's current financial situation (if you are asking for a raise and the company is filing Chapter 11, it may not be possible to make your conversation relevant, no matter what you do)

- Emphasize your competitive edge. For example, if others are making higher wages (the "fairness" appeal), your performance and experience must justify the request. You may be doing the same job, but if everyone in the department has 10 years of experience on you and your last performance review was average (or below) you will have a hard time creating relevance.

- Consider the political impact. If your raise is simply about a salary change, then chances are that it is a quiet matter with little impact on others. But, be careful: If your new salary comes with a new title, how will that news be received by the rest of the team? How will the organization be better off with you in a new role, or a new tax bracket? You must consider the political implications of any change, and take steps to make sure that confidentiality is maintained.

In crafting a NEW Elevator Pitch for a raise, you must also think about the end game. Consider the following:

- What you will do, if the company says, "no"?
- How you want to handle other offers, if you have one (or more) right now. Does it make sense to press your company into a raise?
- Are you willing to walk out the door if it doesn't go your way?
- What's your alternative to your proposal – what will you do?
- Will your boss think of you as a job shopper, if you get the raise and stay on? And, do you even care about being thought of as a "job shopper"?

Consider the following conversation and the implications for both individuals.

SCENARIO: ASKING FOR A RAISE

What NOT to Do...

Employee: Excuse me, sir, may I talk to you?

Boss: Sure, come on in. What can I do for you?

Employee: Well, sir, as you know, I have been an employee of this prestigious firm for over ten years.
Boss: Yes.

Employee: I won't beat around the bush. Sir, I would like a raise. I currently have four companies after me and so I decided to talk to you first.

Boss: A raise? I would love to give you a raise, but this is just not the right time.

Employee: I understand your position, and I know that the current economic downturn has had a negative impact on sales, but you must also take into consideration my hard work, proactiveness, and loyalty to this company for over a decade.

Boss: Taking into account these factors, and considering I don't want to start a brain drain, I'm willing to offer you a ten percent raise and an extra five days of vacation time. How does that sound?

Employee: Great! It's a deal! Thank you, sir!

Boss: Before you go, just out of curiosity, what companies were after you?

Employee: Oh, the Electric Company, the Gas Company, the Water Company, and the Mortgage Company!

"Corporate loyalty" is a bit of an oxymoron in the new economy. Still: Do you want to be seen as a wage mercenary? Or, if you **don't** get what you think you deserve, are you going to go back to your cubicle and take it with a [fake] smile?

When it comes to relevance, you have to think about your options (because your listener always has other options as well). As you think through your pitch, consider the implications – and choose the path that helps you most. Getting another offer on the table may not be a bad thing; just be ready for the potential consequences.

2:00 Your Two-Minute Drill
I've Thought This Through

Your ability to land a raise hinges on how you can prove that "You've thought this through." You have to be prepared for possible outcomes and implications.

So, in two minutes or less, shoot from the hip and see how many of these questions you can answer – and justify:

SCENARIO: ASKING FOR A RAISE

1. Bottom line: How much money do you want?
2. A promotion makes sense for you because...?
3. Is your request reasonable, for your role within your industry?
4. Your raise is best for the organization because...?
5. What will you do for the company, in return for the additional compensation or title?
6. What will you do if you don't get your raise?

What is your answer – and your justification – for each of the six questions above? Can you reply to all six, in two minutes or less?

Pitch Perfect:
Asking for a Raise

Example: Meeting with the Boss

Shannon McGinnis is a project manager at a technology services company in Houston. Her company caters to the energy industry, particularly oil & gas, and business has been doing well. Shannon has asked for a brief meeting with her boss, but didn't go into a lot of detail about the agenda. She has taken on new responsibilities, and wants to talk to her supervisor about a raise.

SHANNON: Tom, thanks for taking the time to talk to me. I wanted to follow up from our conversation a few months ago, when you gave me my performance review. Remember how you said we could talk about my salary, when the economy improves? Well...that's what I'd like to discuss.

First of all, I really appreciate the confidence that you have placed in me. Over these last three years, you have always been willing to give me new responsibilities and that means a lot.

SCENARIO: ASKING FOR A RAISE

Since my performance review I've taken on three new projects, including Permian IV out in Midland. You know that all are ahead of schedule. My work with engineering is going better than ever, and I'm the second-most experienced person in your department.

I really love my work, and I love this company. But I'm concerned that I'm not being valued fairly for my contributions. Business is good, and I'm working hard to make sure it gets better. My wages have been flat for the last year, and out of fairness to me and to the company, I'd like to request a raise. You mentioned that, in a 'normal' economy, a 7% raise would be in order. I hope you agree that my performance merits this increase, and the amount of business I'm responsible for would seem to justify the investment. What would we need to do, to put that pay increase in place?

THE BREAKDOWN

Shannon has done her homework, and she set the stage for this conversation three months ago when her boss put off a discussion of a raise "due to the economy". Patience is more than just a virtue when it comes to what you want – it's a strategy. Shannon knows personally that the financial situation of the company has improved, and her level of responsibility has increased. While Shannon isn't completely certain, there seems to be solid evidence that her work is resulting in greater profitability to the company (finishing projects faster means increased profitability). The scope of her role is the basis for the raise, and she mentions her seniority as well.

PART III: THE SCENARIOS

BE BRIEF: Don't Over-talk Your Raise

One of the key elements that Shannon uses is what my friend, Ellen Bremen, calls "owning your expertise". Ellen is known online as the Chatty Professor – she's a tenured instructor in communications at Highline College in Washington. (Follow her on twitter @chattyprof). Her insight into communication really helped me to understand something about the role of "ownership" when someone asks for a raise. "Our background and expertise are credibility enough," Ellen explains. "We have to own what we know to be true about ourselves." Sometimes, the best way to own something is to be brief about it. "Even in my own communications," Ellen says candidly, "I will think through a decision, get confirmation from people I trust, but then – when it comes time to move forward – I will give off non-verbal clues that make people think that I'm somehow questioning myself." Her advice? Keep it simple, like Shannon.

The reason for the raise is clear – there's no need to go into a dissertation to prove the "why". In fact, over-describing the request doesn't make it stronger.

Keeping Shannon's talent within the company should be a compelling argument for her boss, and her expertise would be hard to replace. "There can be toil and pain before you ask for a raise," Ellen says. "If you rely on connections in your communications style, and relationships are important to you," Ellen says, "put that into your pitch." Play to your strengths, and be brief when your message is clear. Lay your cards out on the table, and see what your boss picks up.

And, if your boss doesn't want to play – maybe it's time to find a new game.

Asking for a raise may be the toughest pitch in the book, especially if the economics don't support what you want. No amount of verbal kung-fu will overcome budgetary restraints, but that doesn't mean you're out of options. Sometimes, going through the "Asking For a Raise" pitch can help you to get clear on your value equation – and where that equation may be most valued.

YOUR HIGHLIGHT REEL
Asking for a Raise

- Understand that one party is interested (you). The other party (the company)? Not so much
- Make your relevant to the company's situation, not your own
- Explain how your raise will benefit the company
- Support your case with performance and productivity metrics
- Watch out for interoffice politics
- Prepare for "No"

An Afterword

When You Make a Real Connection, You Can Make a Real Difference

You now understand how to deliver a message – your message – in a way that is compelling, authentic and relevant. The NEW Elevator Pitch is more than just a strategy for giving a speech – it's a way to create positive change. That change can come in a variety of forms – at home, at work, at school, and more. It's time now to put the NEW Elevator Pitch into action.

So get ready to tell your story, and share the ideas that can make a difference. There's a lot of noise out there. You owe it to yourself, and to your listener, to create the connection you need. That connection is the key; whether you tweet it or tell it, you now have the tools you need for the outcomes you want. It's time to start the conversation.

The NEW Elevator Pitch is your most compelling message, and it deserves to be heard. The audience is listening, so…

Why don't you tell me a little bit about yourself?

Chris

196

Acknowledgements

This book never would have been possible without the guidance and input from the team at Greenleaf Book Group. I especially want to thank my editor, Bill Crawford, for his insights and guidance. To my wife and daughters, I would be lost without your patience and encouragement. Thank you so much. To Jeffrey Hayzlett, author of *Running the Gauntlet*, I want to thank you for the recognition that started me on this path. And to Bill Wallace, Harry Elkin, Dave Peters, and all my friends from Success North Dallas, your encouragement means the world to me. I also want to thank the faculty and staff at Southern Methodist University, the University of North Texas, Texas Christian University, and the dozens of other schools that have heard the story of the NEW Elevator Pitch.

I never knew that a book could be this much work – or be so satisfying. Finally, I want to thank you, the reader. You are the reason I wrote this book, and I hope that it makes a difference in the way that you communicate. I believe your story needs to be heard, and I'm grateful that you took the time to read mine.